GOLD CREEKS & GHOST TOWNS

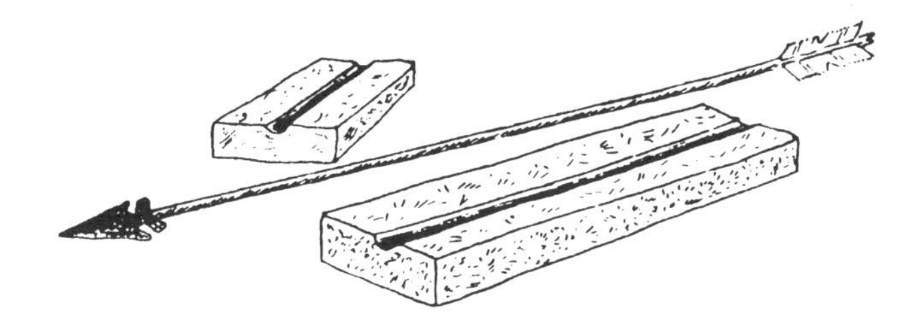

N. L. BARLEE

ISBN 0-88839-988-X

Third edition, fifth printing 2004

Printed in Indonesia—TK PRINTING

Many of the photographs in this book, including those on the back cover, are from the Provincial Archives in Victoria, B.C. The others are from private sources and individuals.
Front cover photo courtesy of the Ministry of Tourism.

Published simultaneously in Canada and the United States by

HANCOCK HOUSE PUBLISHERS LTD.
19313 Zero Avenue, Surrey, B.C. V3S 9R9
(604) 538-1114 Fax (604) 538-2262
HANCOCK HOUSE PUBLISHERS
1431 Harrison Avenue, Blaine, WA 98230-5005
(604) 538-1114 Fax (604) 538-2262
Web Site: www.hancockhouse.com *Email:* sales@hancockhouse.com

TABLE OF CONTENTS

INDEX TO MAPS

Foreword

From the sagebrush, desert country of the southern valleys of the Okanagan and Similkameen across to the high grandeur of the East Kootenay, the southern interior of British Columbia remains an entrancing region.

To some people it is the ghost town country, an area where half a hundred towns stood in another century and names like Sandon, Phoenix, Ferguson and Cascade City were familiar words. To others it is the land of gold creeks, for there was a time when streams like Perry, Granite, Rock and Wild Horse drew thousands of miners in their never ending quest for Eldorado.

Fortunately, some of this area remains relatively unchanged and even today the wilderness is but a glance away and beyond the traveled routes, the trail blazing country still beckons.

For that rather unique breed, those who feel at ease in places far off the beaten path or deep in the back country where the echoes of history are still audible and the atmosphere of half-forgotten eras lingers on, we hope that this book will be enjoyable, for it is for those individuals that it is intended.

Deep in the Tulameen River country, this was the place called Granite City. It was here that gold found by a wandering cowboy named Johnny Chance touched off the Similkameen Rush of 1885.

THE SIMILKAMEEN

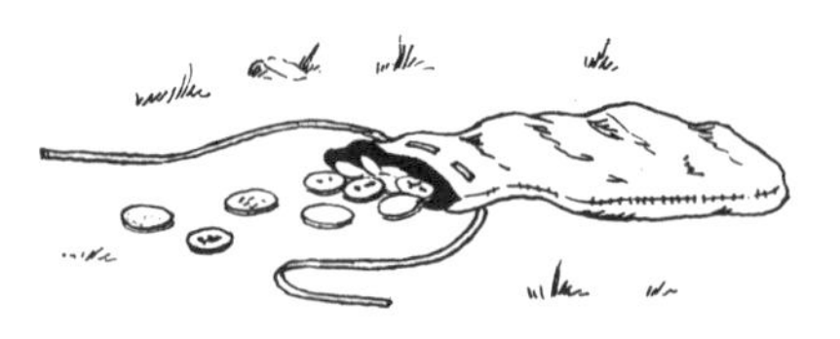

LEATHER POKE WITH SOME SILVER COINS- BLAKEBURN, B.C.

INTRODUCTION

The Similkameen - a land where the passerby may still pan for gold and platinum along the historic placer creeks and rivers of the upper valley or wander through the ghost towns; from gloomy Blakeburn to old Blackfoot, from little known Keremeos Centre to once great Granite City.

Here too, the river may be followed east and south from the majestic canyon country of the west to the wide, sweeping valley along the lower river where ancient Indian trails lead past long abandoned villages like Nlkai'xelox and Ntleuxta'n and landmarks like Soldiers Slide and Standing Rock.

From the Indian country of the south to the gold streams of the west, there remains a panorama of history, for this is the land of the Rainstone, the Nickel Plate and the long lost Spanish Mound - a country for the lone wolf and the footloose, this Similkameen - the "Red Paint" valley.

Some of the wooden grave markers in the Granite City cemetery today.

GHOST TOWNS

TULAMEEN

Before the arrival of the whiteman in the far west, the Similkameen Indians gravitated to this flat which served as a base camp for hunting and a meeting place.

Later, when the fur traders moved into the territory and the brigade trail passed by, it became known as Encampement des Femmes, "camp of the women," so called because the Indian and half-blood women stayed at this location when the men were out trapping or packing along the trail.

In 1885 when the gold rush awakened the Tulameen country, Encampement des Femmes attracted numbers of prospectors and the small town that soon came into being was called Otter Flat. After the gold rush ebbed so did Otter Flat until interest in lode properties in the region gave it a new lease. By 1901 the SIMILKAMEEN STAR was able to report that the provincial government had agreed to survey a townsite at the flat. The survey was carried out and in May of that year Otter Flat was officially designated Tulameen - a name it has retained since that year.

The years haven't been kind to Tulameen, Charles DeBarro's famous log hotel has long since vanished from the scene and so have characters like "Black" Mike and "Lucky" Todd, but there are still some reminders of that colourful era; the Dominion Hotel still looms as large as it did half a century ago and some of the atmosphere of the mining years still clings to this little town deep in the Tulameen country.

The Tulameen General Store and the Dominion Hotel today, two of the last survivors in the old town of Tulameen.

COALMONT

The town once touted as "The City of Destiny...with a population of 10,000 in the near future." Sadly, Coalmont never quite made the grade, in fact it didn't even come close although for decades it was the shipping point for the Blakeburn coal and the headquarters of backers like N. Clark, the editor of the ill-fated COALMONT COURIER which once boasted that it was "the largest newspaper in the province, outside Kamloops, Vernon and Vancouver." Unfortunately, both Coalmont and its Courier never realized their expectations. Now only a few people still live in this quaint little center with its false front buildings and its memories of better years.

The main street of Coalmont in 1970 showing the former Government liquor store and the original post office. Nearby stand the Coalmont Emporium and the Coalmont Hotel, both establishments still serving the region and the occasional passerby.

BLAKEBURN

Only a few people even know the name of this old coal mining town situated in the hill country of the Tulameen valley. Soon after the discovery of coal in the area in the late 19th century Blakeburn came into being and was once described as "the largest, most important coal operation in Princeton district."

As early as 1912, horse drawn wagons were hauling coal from the vast hillside seams down a treacherous, winding road to nearby Coalmont where it was trans-shipped by the Great Northern Railway. Blakeburn really came into its own in 1920 when a three mile aerial tramway was completed to carry coal to the tipple - at the rate of one ton per minute! And by the middle of that decade nearly 300 men were steadily employed in the giant colliery.

Probably the beginning of Blakeburn's demise began abruptly on "Black Wednesday," the 13th day of August of 1930, when a shattering explosion ripped through the No. 4 Mine and left in its wake 45 dead miners. It was a staggering blow to the little town from which it never quite recovered. Although production continued all through the lean years of the depression it was on a steadily decreasing scale and the town never again reached its original prominence.

By 1940, the Collieries closed permanently and all activities at the town ceased. Within a few years the hill community had all but disappeared and today little remains to mark the passing of a town which once claimed a population of 500 and possessed such refinements as a school, a library and even a tennis court. The town of Blakeburn has passed on.

Some of the five hundred coins found in Blakeburn. The majority are now in the E. Gove Collection, the remainder in the Canada West Collection.

GRANITE CITY

Once the largest and most colourful camp in the Tulameen, Granite City came into existence in the summer of 1885 when a sometimes prospector who went by the name of Johnny Chance stumbled across placer gold nuggets on the bedrock of an unnamed tributary of the Tulameen river. The gold was plentiful, often coarse and the diggings shallow.

Soon, news of the strike spread and within weeks growing numbers of men began pouring into the little valley. One of the first arrivals in 1885, an American named Walton Hugh Holmes, described Granite Creek when he first saw it in these words:

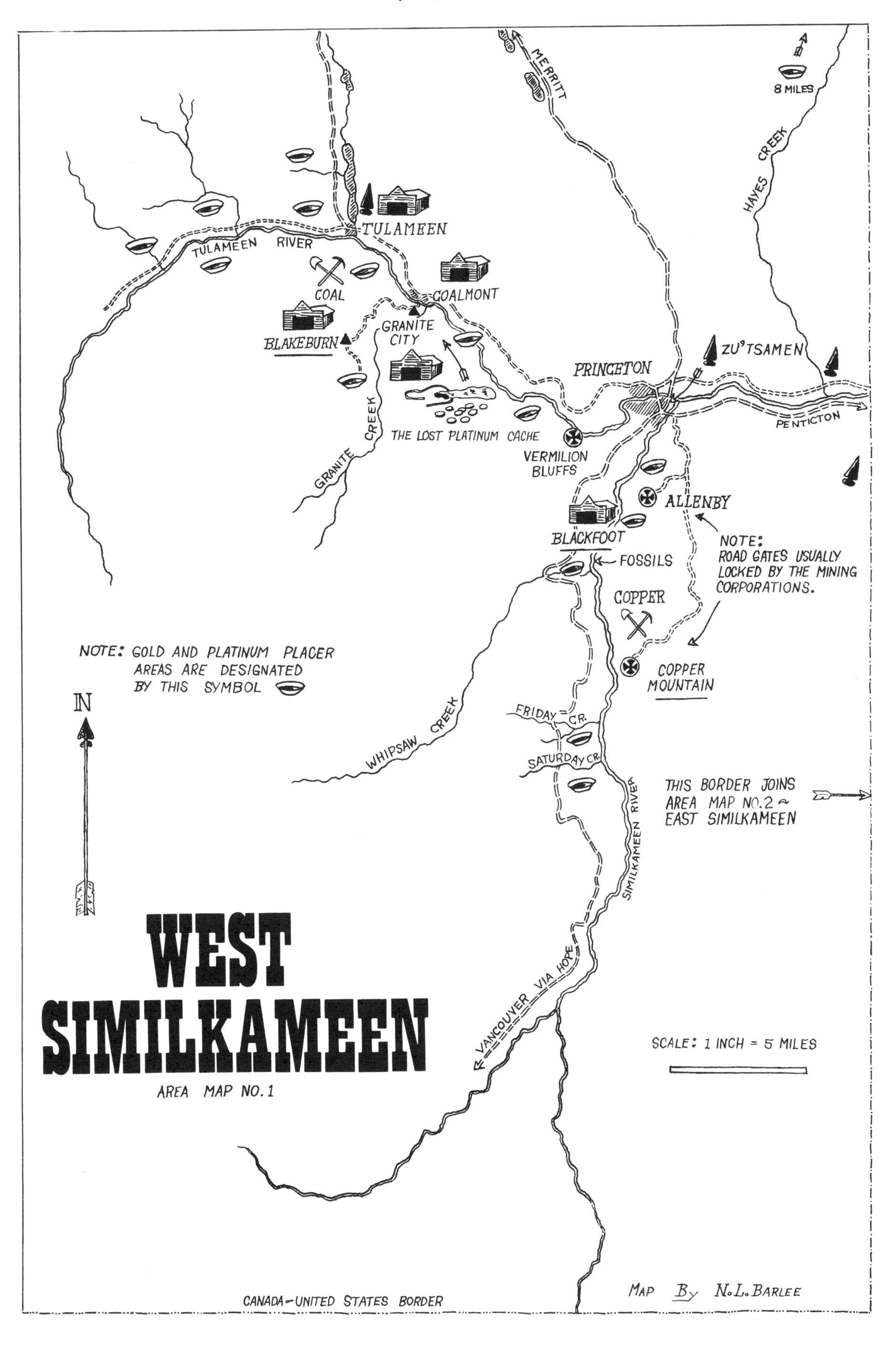
MERRITT
8 MILES
HAYES CREEK
TULAMEEN
TULAMEEN RIVER
COAL
COALMONT
BLAKEBURN
GRANITE CITY
PRINCETON
ZU'TSAMEN
PENTICTON
THE LOST PLATINUM CACHE
VERMILION BLUFFS
GRANITE CREEK
ALLENBY
BLACKFOOT
FOSSILS
NOTE: ROAD GATES USUALLY LOCKED BY THE MINING CORPORATIONS.
COPPER
COPPER MOUNTAIN
NOTE: GOLD AND PLATINUM PLACER AREAS ARE DESIGNATED BY THIS SYMBOL
N
WHIPSAW CREEK
FRIDAY CR.
SATURDAY CR.
SIMILKAMEEN RIVER
THIS BORDER JOINS AREA MAP NO.2 ~ EAST SIMILKAMEEN
WEST SIMILKAMEEN
AREA MAP NO.1
VANCOUVER VIA HOPE
SCALE: 1 INCH = 5 MILES
MAP BY N.L.BARLEE
CANADA-UNITED STATES BORDER

".....when we came in sight of Granite Creek it looked like an ant-hill. Several hundred men of all sorts, saddle horses and pack animals, tents on both sides of the river. What a sight! All available space taken up for tents. Campfires everywhere...."

Before that fall, a hodgepodge collection of log buildings had been thrown up on a bench near the mouth of the creek - this new camp was soon christened Granite City although it was occasionally called Granite Creek or simply Granite.

By the spring of 1886, there were 300 white prospectors and nearly 100 Chinese in the immediate vicinity and Granite City had become a bona fide mining camp. That it grew to respectable proportions was verified by the highly respected VICTORIA COLONIST which on April 21, 1886, was able to report that the camp had:

" 9 general stores, 14 hotels and restaurants, 2 jewelers, 3 bakers, 3 blacksmiths, 2 livery stables, a shoemaker, butcher, chemist, attorney, doctor and 8 pack trains owned in the city. 200 buildings occupy the two main streets - Government and Granite."

Although this report has been questioned, it is generally accepted that in 1886, Granite was larger than any other city in British Columbia

This is Granite City with famous Granite Creek close by. Circa 1890.

except Victoria, Vancouver and New Westminster. Despite its size Granite never built either a church or a school although few of its inhabitants really seemed to miss these attributes, possibly because there were a number of other edifices with diversions of a somewhat different nature among its business establishments on its noisy streets. Strangely, although it had the reputation of a tough town there were few cases of any serious lawbreaking and when a miner occasionally became too rambunctious he was simply installed in the Granite City jail, possibly one of the most unique lockups in the entire west - its windows lacked bars! Nobody, however, is reported to have ever escaped from custody, perhaps because the inmates were unable to squeeze through the jail windows which some farsighted individual had cleverly made rather small - the openings were only one foot square!

Like many old mining towns, Granite had more than its share of real characters. One of them, a judge named Thomas Murphy, was once described in an early issue of the SIMILKAMEEN STAR as being " in Granite so long that he remembers when Mr. Columbus sailed up the Tulameen to discover America."

The future of the camp, however, was tied up with the prosperity of the placer creeks and when they began to play out so did Granite City. By 1895, after a decade of feverish activity, Granite City began to decline and the population, little by little, began to diminish. When, on April 4, 1907, most of the town was destroyed by fire, it was anti-climax for Granite City was finished anyway.

Although the great Cariboo House and a number of log cabins remained standing after the conflagration, the later attempts to rebuild were both half-hearted and unsuccessful for geography and necessity had doomed the camp. A decade later it lay virtually deserted.

Today only a few broken bottles, half a dozen decrepit log buildings and the old cemetery stand on the site which once rang to the sounds of the miners coming in from their claims to live it up in the city known as Granite.

The remains of the city of Granite in 1970.

A few blown bottles from Granite. (Courtesy of the Bradbeer Collection)

BLACKFOOT

A quarter of a century before the celebrated 1885 gold rush to the Similkameen, placer gold had been found in considerable quantity about six miles up the south fork of the Similkameen from Princeton. For a short time an obscure camp graced a flat close to the river. This gold camp, however, soon disappeared and today only the vague indications of the old place called Blackfoot are discernible near the river's edge.

COPPER MOUNTAIN

From a rich outcrop of copper ore accidently discovered by a trapper named James Jameson and his son while out hunting deer in 1884, grew one of the greatest mining camps in the west - Copper Mountain.

The first camps on location were "Volcanic" Brown's and E. Voight's Camp, later combined to form the nucleus of the Granby Company's great Copper Mountain operation.

After over half a century of production, Copper Mountain was finally permanently closed in 1958 and the old town on the site was abandoned to the elements and slowly fell into disuse and decay.

Today Copper Mountain, like old Phoenix in the Boundary country, has fallen victim to open pit mining and the town has virtually vanished. The town once known as Copper Mountain no longer exists.

HEDLEY

Tucked into a shadowy, narrow little canyon and overshadowed by the vertical cliffs of Stemwinder Mountain to the west and the mountain called Nickel Plate to the east is the town they call Hedley.

The Indians knew it by the name Snaizaist, "Striped Rock Place" for they were quick to notice the unusual striations of the bluffs close by. The prospectors edging their way into the valley along the old Dewdney Trail also noticed the vividly coloured cliffs which indicated deposits of ore to their practised eyes and they were not slow to investigate.

By 1894 claims had been staked on Nickel Plate Mountain and by 1898, Jacobson, Johnson, Scott, Wollaston, Arundell and others had located on the mountain, these claims were later to become the basis of the renowned Nickel Plate Mine. In 1899, George Cahill staked the wedge which was to become one of the richest fractions in British Columbia mining history, from this small fraction arose the illustrious Hedley-Mascot Mine.

By the turn of the century, a prosperous mining town had grown up near the mouth of Twenty Mile canyon and the camp was called Hedley.

Within five years the town was booming and grand hotels like the Great Northern and the Similkameen were erected along with others like the Grand Union, Commercial and the New Zealand. Here too, the Bank of British North America saw fit to locate and in short order a number of other new businesses were attracted to the town.

The HEDLEY GAZETTE quickly became the spokesman for the district as the mines on Nickel Plate Mountain came into production. By 1904 the stamp

Hedley in 1906.

The J.A. Schubert General store and post office in Hedley in 1903. One of several general stores in the mining camp.

The first Great Northern passenger train into Hedley. Dec. 23, 1909.

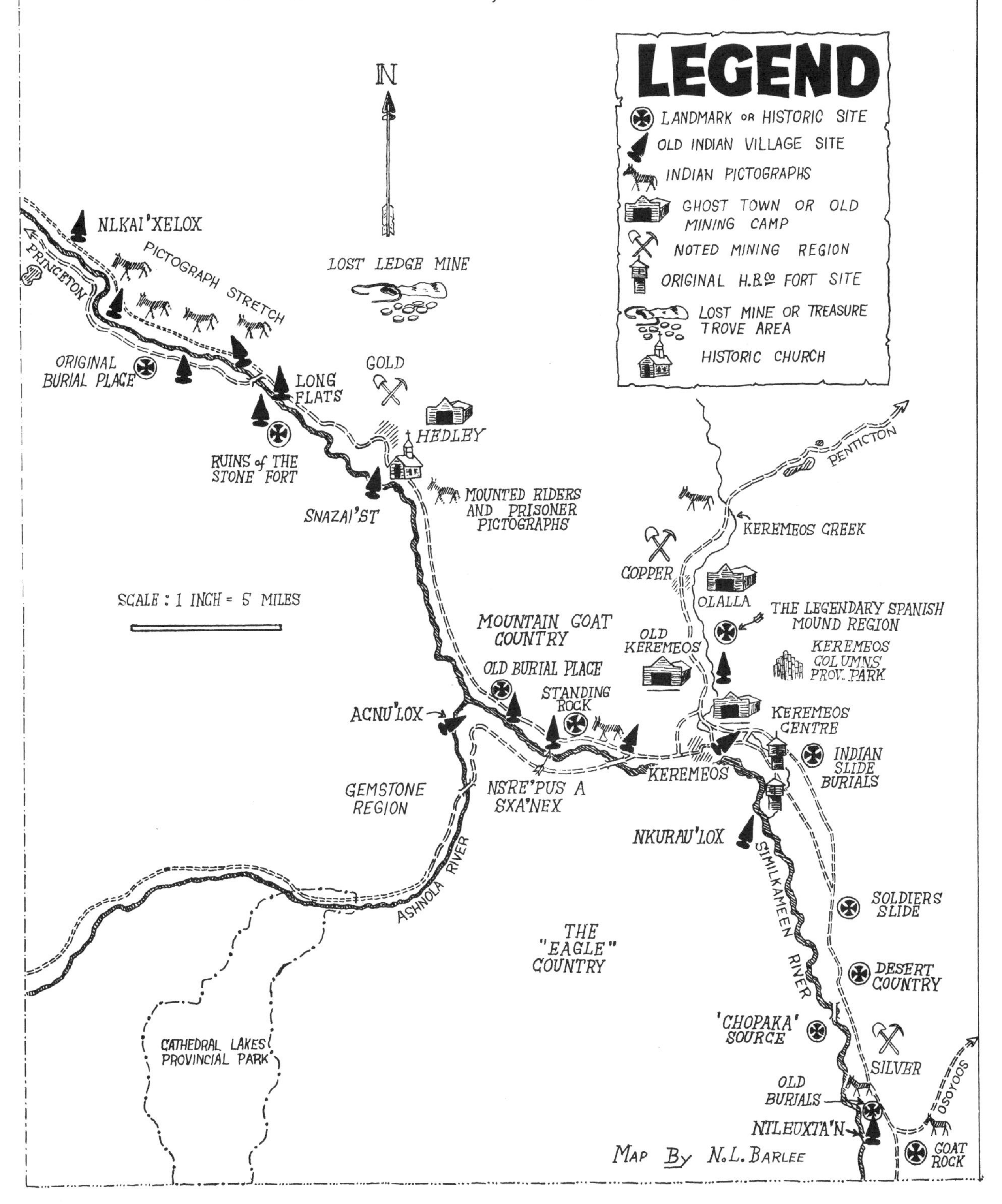
EAST SIMILKAMEEN
AREA MAP NO. 2
AN ORIGINAL MAP SHOWING VARIOUS AREAS of INTEREST, HISTORIC SITES AND GHOST TOWNS.
LEGEND
LANDMARK OR HISTORIC SITE
OLD INDIAN VILLAGE SITE
INDIAN PICTOGRAPHS
GHOST TOWN OR OLD MINING CAMP
NOTED MINING REGION
ORIGINAL H.B.Co FORT SITE
LOST MINE OR TREASURE TROVE AREA
HISTORIC CHURCH
N
NLKAI'XELOX
PRINCETON
PICTOGRAPH STRETCH
LOST LEDGE MINE
ORIGINAL BURIAL PLACE
LONG FLATS
GOLD
HEDLEY
RUINS of THE STONE FORT
SNAZAI'ST
MOUNTED RIDERS AND PRISONER PICTOGRAPHS
PENTICTON
KEREMEOS CREEK
COPPER
OLALLA
THE LEGENDARY SPANISH MOUND REGION
SCALE : 1 INCH = 5 MILES
MOUNTAIN GOAT COUNTRY
OLD KEREMEOS
KEREMEOS COLUMNS PROV. PARK
OLD BURIAL PLACE
STANDING ROCK
ACNU'LOX
KEREMEOS CENTRE
INDIAN SLIDE BURIALS
KEREMEOS
GEMSTONE REGION
NSRE'PUS A SXA'NEX
NKURAU'LOX
SIMILKAMEEN RIVER
ASHNOLA RIVER
SOLDIERS SLIDE
THE "EAGLE" COUNTRY
DESERT COUNTRY
'CHOPAKA' SOURCE
SILVER
CATHEDRAL LAKES PROVINCIAL PARK
OLD BURIALS
NTLEUXTA'N
OSOYOOS
GOAT ROCK
MAP BY N.L. BARLEE

mill was operating full blast and soon the profits and dividends began to pour in. It was the beginning of a long period of unbroken prosperity for the mountaintop mines, for unlike many mining camps, it was a long-lived camp and down through the years it was to prove to be one of the nation's greatest producers.

By 1950, however, the known ore veins were finally exhausted and the mines were forced to close. Although the mines were idled, Hedley didn't die and today waits patiently for another era to dawn, the day when the hillside mines will ring with activity and mining will again be king.

The old Daly Reduction workings just to the east of Hedley today.

KEREMEOS CENTRE AND OLD KEREMEOS

These two old settlements were approximately two miles north-east of present day Keremeos. Old Keremeos was established in the 1890's but an inadequate water supply forced removal of the town to another site on a bench above Keremeos Creek barely half a mile to the south-west. The new town was called Keremeos Centre and quickly became a mining supply depot and stagecoach stop until the townsite was again shifted in 1906 to the present location of Keremeos.

A decade ago six structures including the impressive Central Hotel, the old livery stable and the Inglewood Supply could be seen at Keremeos

Typical of the stagecoaches in the Similkameen was Welby's "flier."

The site of Old Keremeos today - little left but sagebrush and sand.

Centre. Now only the lonely grave of John Chuchuaskin Ashinola watches over the empty main street. And at Old Keremeos, a forlorn and withering apricot tree stands vigil on the windswept flats where the first town called Keremeos once stood.

Some blown bottles from Old Keremeos and Keremeos Centre. From the fine Parsons collection in Keremeos.

OLALLA

The unusual name of this little stopping place was derived from the Salish Indian word "soopolalie" which was the name given to a favourite berry bush found in the vicinity. This word was later shortened and corrupted to "Olalla."

At one time the area was a promising mining region with a number of copper showings along the steep hillsides. In those heady years many a prospector scoffed at offers lower than $10,000 for a claim and assays on the Elkhorn, Bullion Hill and other groups of claims indicated a great camp. By 1907, however, it was finally becoming obvious that values didn't extend to depth and the earlier estimates began to be revised.

Fletcher R. Parsons, an honest field man for the British Columbia Mining and Smelting Company in Olalla wrote in a letter dated Nov. 21, 1907, to the head office in New York, complaining:

"....I will not be quoted in the NEW YORK JOURNAL as saying that the wonderful outlook of the B.C.M. & S. Co. exceeds anything else in the world - it don't by a long shot."

So the smelter plan was reluctantly filed away and Olalla with its one main hotel, assay office and store gradually slipped into oblivion.

Today, few reminders of the mining years remain in Olalla after the 1963 fire which swept away much of its history and only a few abandoned tunnels indicate that there was once a mining camp nearby.

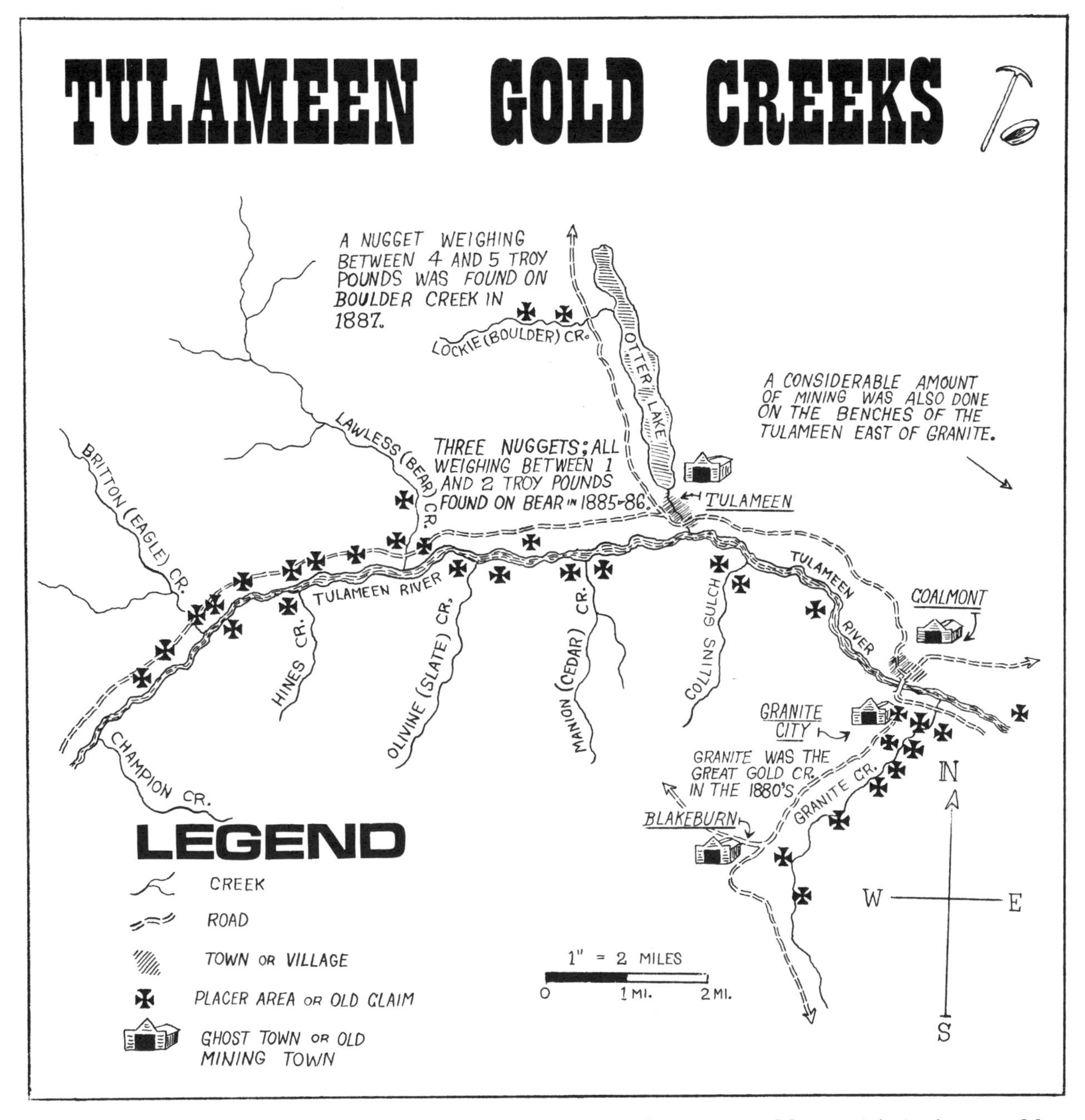

The map on this page shows part of the Tulameen valley which is really a western extension of the Similkameen. This is where the 1885 Gold Rush began. The majority of the gold creeks have been placed on this map with both the old and present names. It should also be remembered that a great amount of placer platinum was also taken out of this area in the early years. The larger ghost and shadow towns have also been placed on the map as have the roads and some historic details. A more detailed scale map of this region (sheet 92 H/NE "Tulameen, B.C.") is available from provincial government offices in the interior at a price of $1.00. Caution should be exercised when taking the road west of the town of Tulameen as this road up the river is often not negotiable, especially in the spring and winter. Other roads in the general area should be checked out with local inhabitants before attempts are made to travel on them.

GOLD CREEKS

● Ashnola River - Although it has been variously reported that placer gold has been recovered on this river, the mining reports in the archives at Victoria do not support this. It is possible to pan out colours near the mouth of the Ashnola where it joins the Similkameen. The colours are very fine. Prospects: poor indeed.

● Britton (Eagle) Creek - A tributary of the Tulameen River which was originally known as Eagle Creek. Discovered in 1885 when a significant amount of gold was recovered from the creek - mainly close to the mouth. Worked quite extensively over the years it has also yielded a great deal of placer platinum. The last major find was by Garnet Sootheran in 1926 when a considerable amount of both placer gold and platinum were found. Although this stream, like most of the others in the area, has been well worked there are still interesting possibilities for the week-end miner. This creek is eight miles south-west of the old town of Tulameen. It is possible to reach this stream by road. Prospects: intriguing - watch for pay-streaks that the original miners couldn't reach. The benches in other years have often proven profitable although the immediate area has been well prospected.

Collins Gulch - Also discovered in 1885 and worked by both the whites and Chinese. According to the mining reports, the early returns from this creek were quite good but unlike some of the other gold creeks nearby the

Some prospectors leading their packhorses across "the Bridge" over the Tulameen River near Granite Creek. Circa 1890.

diggings were exhausted quite rapidly. This stream flows into the Tulameen River from the south side and is located approximately 1½ miles east of the village of Tulameen. Crossing the river to get to the creek presents some problems. Prospects: not as good as many of the other streams in the region.

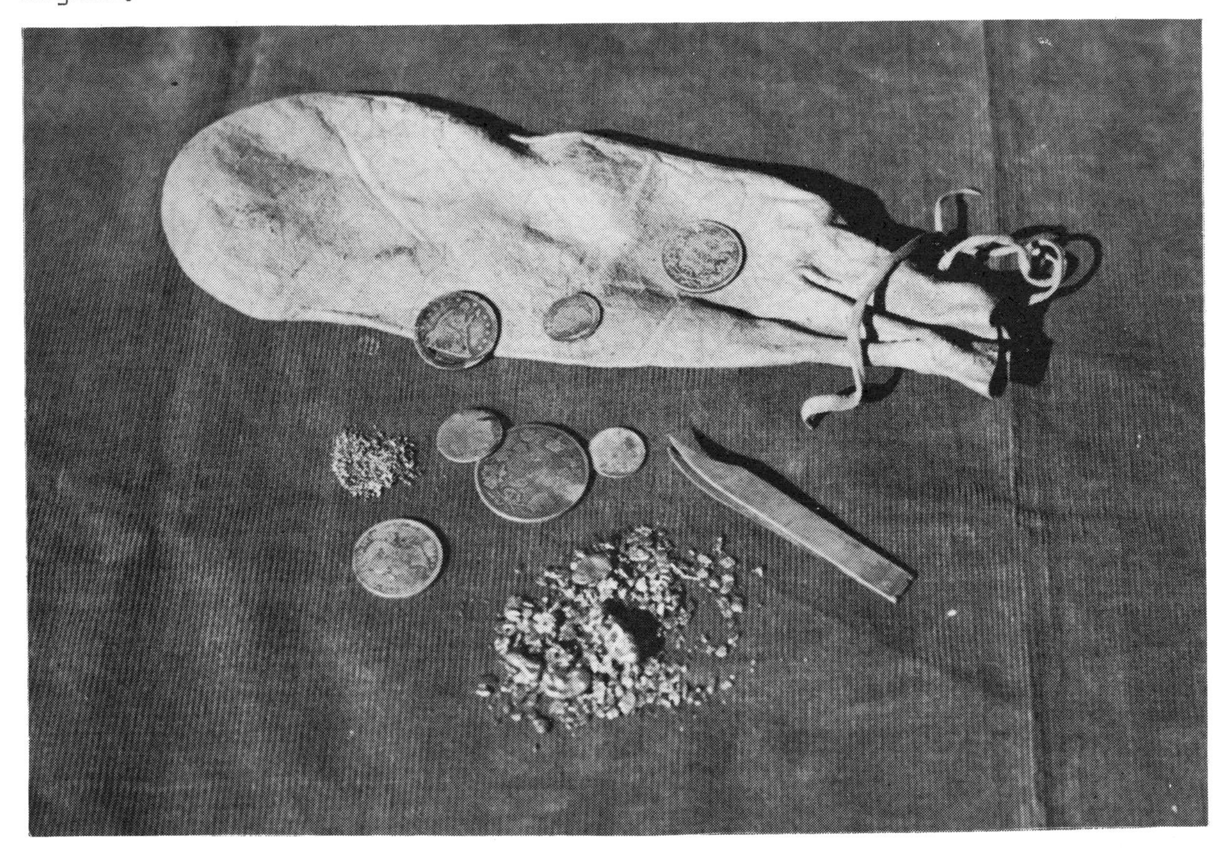

Gold and platinum from interior creeks with tweezers, coins and a gold poke.

● Granite Creek - A tributary of the Tulameen River and the most renowned placer creek in the area. Granite was reputedly discovered in 1885 by John Chance although there is some evidence that it was actually found in the fall of 1884 by Briggs, Bromley and a third partner. This stream flows north into the Tulameen and joins that river approximately 1½ miles to the east of Coalmont. Estimates vary greatly but it is generally assumed that Granite Creek has yielded more than $500,000 in placer gold since its discovery. It is also recognized as one of the best of the placer platinum creeks in the region with that metal occasionally equalling the weight of the gold recovered although it generally approximates one-half of the gold weight found. Both the gold and platinum are coarse and run to 875 fine. Nuggets of $50 value were not unusual in the early years. This creek was worked extensively by both whites and Chinese and was hydraulicked near its mouth in the 1890's. Prospects: Only reasonable as it has been quite thoroughly prospected by innumerable experienced prospectors. In places a very difficult stream to work with the best ground found from its mouth upstream for about five miles. A few possibilities for snipers and some individuals feel that the benches have not been as thoroughly tested as they should have been. An historic gold creek which has been well worked.

An abandoned flume from a placer operation near Coalmont. Beyond are the Tulameen river and a decaying pumphouse once used in the hydraulicking.

● Hayes (Five Mile) Creek - Formerly called Five Mile Creek, this stream flows south into the Similkameen and joins with that river approximately five miles east of Princeton. Placer gold was discovered in this creek in 1887. The gold is invariably fine and nuggets above 50¢ difficult to come across. Prospects: Not good although it has not been as well prospected as other more well known gold streams in the region.

● Lawless (Bear) Creek - Discovered in 1885 and originally called Bear Creek. In the first two years T.G. Tunstall, the gold commissioner, reported that nuggets of $320, $400 and $415 value were taken out. It was worked by both Chinese and whites and the gold recovered was unusually coarse. It was also one of the best of the platinum creeks. Lawless flows south-east into the Tulameen River about four miles west of the old village of Tulameen. Prospects: An exceptionally interesting creek despite the fact that it has been well prospected. If any finds are to be made on this placer stream they should be well worthwhile.

● Lockie (Boulder) Creek - Once known as Boulder Creek, this stream is on the west side of Otter Lake. Generally spotty with some spectacular finds. The best ground was about a mile upstream from its mouth although some places above the canyon were good. This was a favourite creek of the Chinese who held much of its length for some years. The largest nugget in the Similkameen-Tulameen district was recovered from Lockie in 1887 when a Chinese miner working for a Chinese company unearthed a nugget weighing between four and five troy pounds and valued at $900. The existence of this huge nugget was kept secret until it was sold to Wells, Fargo and Company, who placed it on exhibition in their bank in Victoria. Lockie has also produced a considerable amount of placer platinum. Prospects: Better than most of the other creeks in the area with some chance of discovering previously untouched paystreaks above the canyon.

● Manion (Cedar) Creek - Discovered during the 1885 rush, this stream was originally called Cedar Creek. Found approximately 1½ miles up-river from the village of Tulameen, it flows into the Tulameen River from the south. It was worked extensively in the early years and much of it has been ground-sluiced. A considerable amount of coarse platinum has been recovered from this creek, some of it weighing from 2 to 4 pennyweights. The gold is also often coarse with nuggets exceeding 2 ounces not unusual especially prior to 1900. Prospects: difficult to get at as it is on the south side of the river. It could prove worthwhile to the patient miner who is willing to research the history of this creek in order to prospect ground which has not been well worked.

● Olivine (Slate) Creek - Once one of the richer creeks in the region, it is still often known by its old name, Slate. Discovered in 1885, the early prospectors worked this creek for decades with some excellent results. Both gold and platinum are obtained from the gravels with the gold

This photograph shows the Placer Development Company of America's placer operation on the Tulameen River. Notice the miner and the hand car in the center of the picture. The water is being flumed over the workings.

often being coarse and nuggets, especially in the discovery years, quite commonplace. Olivine flows into the Tulameen from the south side and is about 3 miles up the river from Tulameen village. Prospects: again hard to get into which usually means that it has more possibilities than the more easily accessible creeks. An historically good creek which should be prospected with considerable care if good ground is to be located.

An abandoned prospector's sod roofed cabin along the Similkameen River.

● Saturday Creek - This stream is located up the Similkameen River some 15 river miles from Princeton. Both Saturday and Friday Creeks (which is located just downstream) flow into the Similkameen from the west and were known as good gold creeks, often yielding coarse gold. The benches on the west side of the river were quite productive and have been worked on and off for decades with varying success.

● Similkameen River - Gold was reportedly discovered on this noted placer river in 1858 but possibly as early as 1853. Although it has a reputation for being somewhat spotty in places, the Similkameen is yielding excellent gold even today. The most productive section of the river has always been from 3 miles east of Princeton up-river to the mouth of Whipsaw Creek, although gold has been recovered both up-river and down-river from this stretch. This river has been worked semi-continuously for slightly more than 100 years and in all probability it will be worked for another century. Both bedrock and lower benches have produced well and even an ill-fated dredging operation obtained some interesting results. The gold tends to be somewhat coarser between Princeton and Whipsaw although nuggets above ten pennyweight were rare even in the 19th century. The depth to bedrock varies considerably although in several places snipers have done quite well. Prospects: rather amazingly good considering the amount of work done on this river. Between the Forks (Princeton) and Whipsaw the best ground is usually found on the west side of the river. The platinum usually runs to approximately one-eighth of the gold weight recovered. A most fascinating placer river.

● Siwash Creek - This stream flows into Hayes Creek approximately 3 miles west of Jellicoe and slightly over 20 miles north-east of Princeton. Rough edged gold has been recovered in small quantity by a number of prospectors who have worked this creek. The best ground is from 5 to 8 miles up from its mouth, with most of the work concentrated in the area between Teepee and Galena Creeks both of which enter Siwash from the east. There are a number of low benches ranging from 10 to 50 feet above the stream which were probably old channels once. Prospects: a logical creek for a small hydraulic operation with the gravel in some places running as high as $3 per cubic yard. The gold, however, invariably runs fine with nuggets over 50¢ rather scarce. This is a creek which should be prospected thoroughly although good ground is probably at a premium.

Gold was first discovered along the Similkameen River at a place called California Flats prior to 1859. Soon a dozen or more cabins were erected on the spot and the settlement called Blackfoot came into being. This is all that remains of the old camp today which is so far off the main road that even the bottle collectors have missed it.

● Tulameen River - Along with Granite Creek and the Similkameen River, the Tulameen was an equivalent producer. Originally called the Vermilion or sometimes the Rouge, it was being worked by placer miners in 1860 and possibly earlier. Varying in richness, the Tulameen has yielded both gold and platinum from the forks at Princeton up-river to Champion Creek. In places this river was astonishingly rich in both metals, in other spots it was relatively barren. The best paying ground was from a point about 4 miles down from Granite Creek up to Britton (Eagle) Creek. This was the stretch where the greatest amount of both noble metals were recovered. Like the Similkameen, the Tulameen has been exposed to hydraulicking and dredging as well as the more usual methods of placer mining. Although the gold was often coarse, especially on the upper river, nuggets found seldom exceeded 2 ounces. Prospects: a river with this length of potential ground cannot easily be ignored although it has been well prospected. The benches have been worked, often with good results, and probably still offer the best possibilities.

● Whipsaw Creek - This creek flows into the Similkameen River from the west and is approximately 6 miles up-river from Princeton. Much gold has come from this stream with the best ground from its mouth up-stream for a little over a mile although various other parts of the creek have also been productive. In the early years nuggets weighing up to 2 ounces were not unusual. Whipsaw, however, is a difficult stream to work; many of the boulders encountered are of staggering size and the terrain through which the creek flows does not lend itself to easy operations. Prospects: still a creek which has potential although the problems which will probably be encountered may prove difficult to overcome.

One of the earliest photographs taken of Vermilion Forks (Princeton).

INDIAN COUNTRY

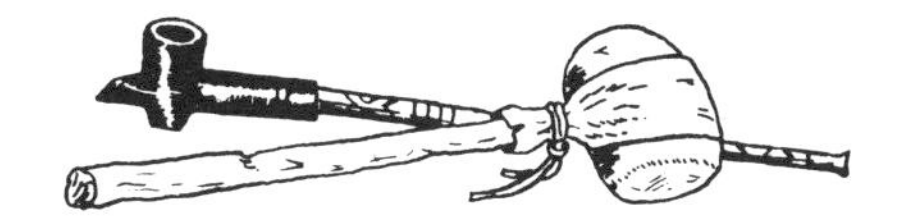

This was the "red paint" valley and the "eagle" country of a vanished era, for it was in this remote region that both highly valued face paint and eagle feathers were obtained by the Plains Indians in trade with the local Similkameen.

The Similkameen country, according to the authoritative James Teit, was originally inhabited by the Stuwi'x, an Athapascan Indian tribe which gave way to the Thompson bands pressing into the northern part of the valley and the Okanagan edging in from the south and east. From these two Salishan groups came the stock of the present-day Similkameen.

These Indians ranged the length of the valley, north from the "red paint" or Zu'tsamen band's territory near the confluence of the Tulameen and Similkameen rivers south to Ntleuxta'n near the international border.

In the 19th century, at the height of their power before they were decimated by smallpox, the tribe evidently numbered slightly over 300 and even as late as 1900 was able to muster nearly 150 members.

Since then, however, the once proud Similkameen have been drastically reduced in number, but the valley, especially beyond the travelled routes,

The place the Indians once knew as "Snaizaist" or Striped Rock Place, today it is called Chuchuewa and lies just to the east of the old mining town of Hedley. This was an historic camping-ground of the Similkameen Indians and even now there are sweat houses and other indications of past habitation in the vicinity. The church on the hill was standing when James Teit passed this way in 1904 and had been standing for some time then.

is remarkably like it was a century or more ago - the mountain goats still pick their cautious way along the sheer slopes of the high country, and the sagebrush, the talus slides and the winding river continue to command the valley below. In many places it is still the west of the past, an almost forgotten yesterday when the Similkameen Indians held undisputed possession of this mountain valley.

The place called Long Flats; a rendezvous used by the Similkameen Indians when trading with the Plains Indians who traveled to this spot to obtain both eagle feathers and red ochre for face paint. On the far side of the river the original Plains Indian village site stood on the clearing to the left; the Similkameens camped on the near side. Now today's highway runs close by this camp of the past where only a few artifacts indicate that it ever existed.

The Similkameen valley has some of the most magnificent displays of Indian pictographs in the west - the "pictograph stretch" section alone containing nearly fifty sets of paintings.

Sadly, some of the pictographs which once graced the valley may no longer be seen because they have been defaced or chipped away by vandals who are unable to realize that Indian paintings are one of the few visible links with the past which remain almost unchanged year after year but once they are destroyed they are lost forever, for the hand that painted them has long vanished from the scene.

The sketches on the following page are from a few of the memorable sets in the Similkameen, many of them hard by the original Indian horse trail which in other years ran the length of the valley.

Some pictographs along the "pictograph stretch," west of Hedley.

The memorable "Drowned Warrior" paintings in the same area.

The following page shows photographs of both the Parsons Collection and a picture of a pictograph site in the east Similkameen.

The artifacts in the Parsons Collection represent only a fraction of their entire collection and are typical of Similkameen Indian artifacts. They were collected over a number of years from numerous sites like Long Flats, Wolfe Lake, Keremeos and other sites along the Similkameen River.

The next photograph shows a rocky wall in which Indian pictographs are visible. An ancient Indian trail once passed through this region east of Olalla and Indian hunters paused to paint symbols on this rocky face and the pictographs are still legible more than a century later.

Some Indian artifacts from the Doug Parsons Collection in Keremeos.

One of numerous pictograph sites in the Similkameen country.

"Goat Rock" - deep in the desert country of the south Similkameen. This was nature's landmark and the Indians of yesterday knew it well. For here the trails divided; one led south, the one the proud horse stealers would take, one headed east through the Richter Pass country - this was the one that the bison hunters would take on their dangerous forays into Blackfoot territory east of the Rockies. The trail north led deep into the remote upper Similkameen country - the "eagle" and "red paint" land. (below)

Several items found by Bruce MacFayden near an old rendezvous on the famous Dewdney Trail north-west of Goat Rock. Amongst the artifacts is a fine elbow pipe which was sometimes referred to as a "Chopaka" after the place nearby where the black soapstone material was obtained. These pipes were so highly regarded that they were traded far into the Great Plains. Also pictured is a 19th century English gold sovereign which was found on the Dewdney Trail on the Kohler Ranch property north of the rendezvous.
(top photograph on the following page)

Some artifacts from the "Canada West" Collection. The majority of these items were recovered from the Similkameen country some years ago and indicate that the Similkameen Indians had become an extremely wealthy tribe through trading with other interior tribes and the Plains Indians. The necklace in the center is one of the finest ever found in the valley and is composed of dentalia, which served as the trade money of the west, and prized blue trade beads, probably obtained from the H.B.Co.'s post at Keremeos which was established in 1860. (lower photograph same page)

Goat Rock - the trail marker.

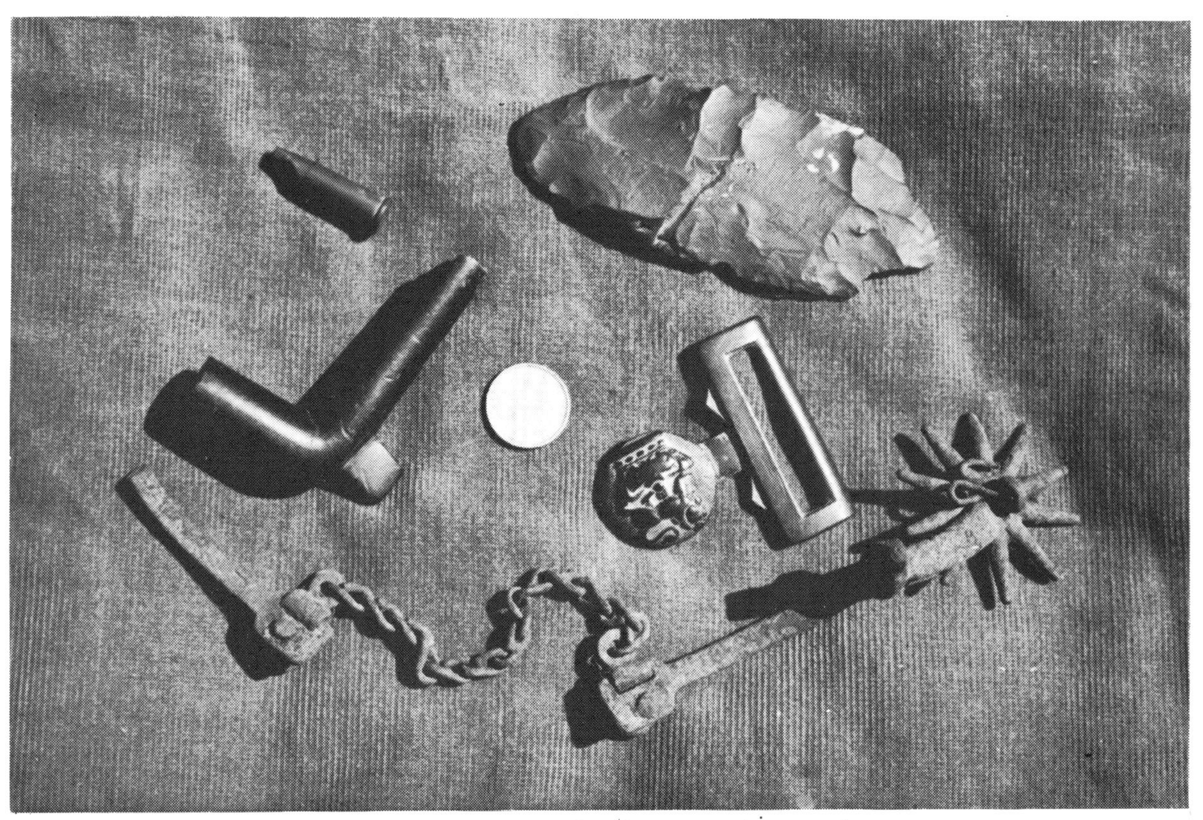

"Chopaka" - the black soapstone pipe.

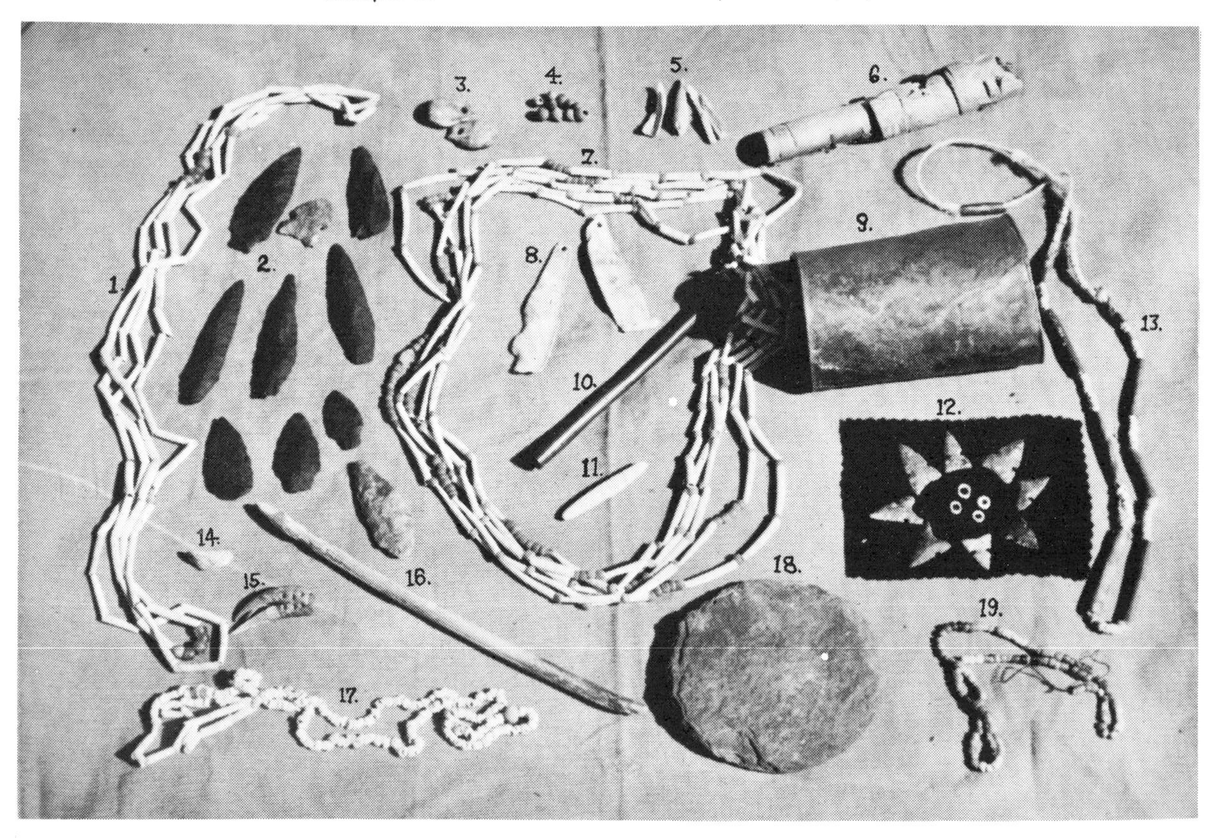

Similkameen Indian artifacts from the "Canada West" Collection.

TREASURE TROVE

Although it is generally conceeded that a great percentage of the many treasure tales and lost mine stories are either purely fictitious or so highly embellished that all relevant information has been obscured, there are still, however, certain tales which due to historical background or other significant data deserve to be related.

There are two stories out of a vast number circulating in the valley of the Similkameen which are somewhat plausible and may actually exist, for they are based on an impressive array of rather interesting evidence.

THE LEGEND OF THE OLD SPANISH MOUND

This is a legend which has survived in the valley almost unchanged for well over a century, and even today there are older Indians in the Similkameen who will swear to its validity.

Although this story has been the subject of several articles, there are a few more clues which have been unearthed which lend even greater credence to this unique treasure tale.

Copper Indian armour-plate recovered from an ancient Indian burial near Keremeos. Each piece is fashioned from heavy copper and is perforated at the top. To the right is an iron spearpoint. (Parsons Collection)

The renowned "Prisoner Paintings" with the puzzling mounted riders close by. These pictographs may be one of the last surviving links to the old Spanish expedition theory.

The following account first appeared in N.L. Barlee's "Similkameen - the Pictograph Country." With the exception of several additions the story is nearly the same as the original version.

According to the old legend, the Spanish Mound is a low-lying grassy mound in which are buried the weapons and armour and remains of long-dead Spanish soldiers, members of an ill-fated expedition which was ambushed and annihilated by the Similkameen Indians almost two centuries ago.

The legend relates a story concerning an expedition which came into the Similkameen long before "King George's Men" arrived in the valley.

The Indians say that sometime near the middle of the 18th century, a band of strange-looking men with white faces and wearing "metal" clothes marched up the Similkameen from the south and set up camp near Keremeos. They remained at this campsite until an altercation erupted between an Indian and a soldier; the quarrel quickly turned into a small scale battle between the natives and the whites. In this fray, the Spanish managed to inflict heavy losses on the Indians, and afterwards the Spaniards, along with several Indian prisoners taken as carriers retreated to the north-east and disappeared up the valley of Keremeos Creek.

Continuing up this creek, over the divide and then down the Shingle Creek draw, they crossed over the flats at the foot of Okanagan Lake near Penti'kten then followed the lake north along the old east-side trail to

Nxokosten and established a camp close to a little creek slightly to the north of that ancient Indian village near present-day Kelowna. Here they built strong permanent quarters and wintered.

The following spring, for reasons unknown, although probably because their ranks had been decimated by either disease or Indian hostility, they left the area and retraced their steps southward. At any rate, the column with their numbers somewhat reduced from the summer before appeared again in the valley near the upper reaches of Keremeos Creek.

Several days later, so the legend states, they marched out of the hills and camped on a small flat overlooking Keremeos Creek near where that stream enters the valley proper. Forewarned, the Similkameen tribe waited and when the unsuspecting Spaniards finally struck camp and moved off down the valley they were suddenly ambushed in overwhelming numbers; and after a sharp and bloody battle the Indians slaughtered them to the last man.

After this epic struggle, according to the legend, the Similkameen then buried the despised white strangers; with most of their armour and weapons in a small mound somewhere between the last Spanish camp and the Keremye'us Indian village, and they lie there to this day, in this long lost and unmarked burial place - the legendary "Spanish Mound."

In examining this legend it must be noted that there are no official Spanish records to substantiate the theory that a Spanish column actually

Beyond the deserted cabins in the background, Keremeos Creek enters the valley. This was the region where the legendary massacre of the Spanish Column took place.

did penetrate inland this far north. However, some evidence exists which merits consideration. This is the evidence:

● Old steel weapons have been unearthed in the vicinity of Keremeos and some of these do not appear to be the usual trade items. It is possible that they were traded inland, but if that was the case, why were they concentrated almost exclusively in the Keremeos area?

● Various pictographs in the valley depict mounted whites. One set (see photograph) portrays horsemen which, judging by their headgear, could be Spaniards. Was this painting originally inspired by the Spanish column? Another set of pictographs (same photograph) shows four Indians chained or roped together and surrounded by quadrupeds (which closely resemble dogs). DeSoto and other Spaniards did, in fact, often force captive Indians to act as carriers on their expeditions and usually chained them together and guarded them with vicious dogs. The dogs in the pictograph are portrayed with their mouths open, indicating that they are barking. They are also surrounding the prisoners. Are they actually a pack of Spanish fighting hounds? Is this the explanation of the "Prisoner Paintings?"

● The discovery of rare Indian armour made of hammered copper plate (see photgraph) in an old Indian grave near Keremeos. The armour is perforated and remarkably similar to Spanish mail. Was this Indian armour copied from old Spanish mail? If not, where did they get the idea? It is reasonable to assume that none of the employees of the Hudson's Bay Company or the North West Company or the free traders wore armour in the 19th century. Therefore the Indians did not get the idea from the fur traders.

● The physical appearance of the Similkameen also deviates slightly from the other Indian tribes in the neighbouring regions. They were generally taller and finer-boned than other Salishan tribes and they also possessed the almost unique ability to pronounce an "r," (Keremeos) a letter which was virtually unpronouncable for other tribes of the interior and which, incidently, occurs frequently in many Spanish words. Can the differences be attributed to their fraternization with the legendary Spanish column?

● The discovery in 1863, near Mill Creek north-east of Kelowna, of the foundations of a then crumbling and ancient building whose cedar logs had been shaped with iron axes and had been the work of a number of men. This massive structure (35' by 75'), whose size and design indicated that it had been used by a large number of men and horses. Neither the North West Company nor the Hudson's Bay Company established permanent large quarters in that area at any time. Who did then? Was this structure used by the old Spanish expedition?

● Historical records are extant which list the names of several Spanish ships which were wrecked close to the mouth of the Columbia River in the 18th century. Indian folklore of the area states that some of the whites survived. If so, did these Spaniards strike inland and northward in search of the old Spanish goals, "Eldorado" or "The Seven Cities of Cibola?"

● Some years ago a piece of highly polished turquoise was recovered in an old burial in Okanagan Falls. Archaeologists state that this is the only instance of turquoise being found in an Indian grave in the province. Was this turquoise once in the possession of a Spanish soldier in the legendary Spanish column?

The evidence is circumstantial but it is also highly intriguing. The old mystery remains unsolved. Did the Spanish actually march through the Similkameen almost two centuries ago and did they meet their fate in the narrow valley north of Keremeos?

THE LOST PLATINUM CACHE

The complete details of this treasure story have been previously printed in Canada West Magazine. The main particulars are included in the following account.

In the heart of the platinum country lies Granite City. The buried cache reputedly lies close to this abandoned placer camp.

Several treasure tales out of the Tulameen region mention platinum, the most interesting of these accounts is the story of The Lost Platinum Cache of Granite City.

When the Tulameen Gold Rush began in 1885, the early arrivals on the creeks came across an unusual silvery coloured metal which was recovered along with the gold. This new metal had many of the properties of the yellow metal; it was heavy, it was recovered by the same methods, it was found in the same paydirt, it had a brilliant lustre and it was also a "noble" metal. Soon the miners dubbed the unknown metal "white gold."

Prospectors by their very nature are an unusual breed and it was not illogical that while the majority of the hundreds of miners in the valley cursed the strange metal and discarded it, a few curious argonauts began to collect it. The most persistent of these men was a Scandinavian by the name of Johanssen. This individual, during his two year stint at Granite Creek - the most famous of all the gold creeks in the Tulameen, reportedly saved more than 300 ounces of the white metal.

The "white gold" was, of course, platinum, a rare metal which occurs in quantity in only two placer areas in the world and one of these areas is the Tulameen.

Like all gold creeks, Granite's shallow diggings soon became depleted and Johanssen decided to move on to the Kootenays. In a quandry as to what to do about his hoard of platinum before leaving, he finally decided to bury it and reputedly cached it in a battered and ancient bucket, which the old-timers swear, was buried in a shallow spot somewhere south of his cabin and visible from the cabin door.

Unluckily, Granite City was razed by a fire in 1907 and along with most of the cabins in town, Johanssen's dwelling was levelled - with it went the key to the location of the treasure.

So, the platinum cache is probably still there, close to $50,000 in white gold, lying in its secret hiding place near that once famous creek and the ghost town known as Granite.

Again there are certain historical and geological facts which tend to add plausibility to this story:

● Only the Tulameen River country of British Columbia and the Amur River in Russia carry appreciable amounts of placer platinum. Government sources estimate that approximately 15,000 ounces of this precious metal have been recovered in the Tulameen since 1885.

● It is well known that many of the early miners along the Tulameen River and its tributaries discarded great quantities of the rare metal in the years between 1885 and 1900, an era when the strange metal was generally considered worthless. T.G. Tunstall, the gold commissioner for Tulameen, stated in 1887 - "It is a remarkable fact that many thousands of ounces of this rare metal has been thrown away..., in consequence of .... as to its true value. Last year... it commanded only 50¢ per ounce."

● A number of miners like Kong Huey, a well known Chinese headman, also hoarded platinum and there are numerous stories of the Chinese secreting varying amounts of platinum in the region. Unfortunately, few details are available.

● Even past the turn of the century platinum was regarded as an oddity, held in such low esteem that there are residents living today in the area who remember their childhood days when they had their own little pokes of white gold and considered the metal virtually valueless.

● It was standard practice during the depression of the 1930's to burn down the old, abandoned prospector's cabins in the area and then pan the ashes in order to recover the platinum which had been thrown away prior to 1900. A number of individuals made a living doing this at that time.

● Finally, the mining records indicate that the greatest amount of placer platinum recovered in the Tulameen was from Granite Creek, the very stream which the Scandinavian worked in his years in the valley. So, although the story has some flaws it is still quite possible that the lost platinum cache lies undetected in its original hiding place in the remote valley of the Tulameen.

A general view of the mining camp of Fairview in 1899. Once the metropolis of the south Okanagan, today a forgotten and forlorn sagebrush covered flat in the arid hills of the south country.

THE OKANAGAN

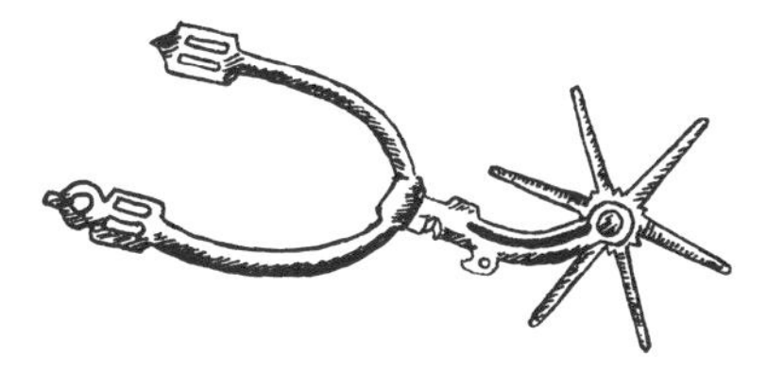

SPUR ~ SOUTH OKANAGAN COUNTRY

INTRODUCTION

The Okanagan - a natural trough in the interior plateau; a chain of lakes stretching south from Great Okanagan and unforgettable Kalamalka to the border lake called Osoyoos, and in between, the old Indian country.

An area where the wanderer can still see the land as it once was; from the hot, lonely desert country of Inkameep to McIntyre Creek's haunted canyon, from the Bighorn country of Vaseux Lake to the distant Greystokes. And here and there, ghost towns of the past; wind swept Fairview and old Cherryville, forgotten Mineola and restored O'Keefe.

Although the gold creeks like Harris, Bear, Mission and Cherry have long passed their peak, the atmosphere stays on and even today a paystreak or occasional nugget is uncovered along these once historic streams where the placer miners of a century ago toiled.

Indian villages like Nkoma'peleks and Tselo'tsus have been deserted these many years but this is still the land of N'ha-a-Itk, the demon of the big lake, eerie Painted Canyon and legendary Battle Bluff, this valley called the Okanagan - this land of many colours.

The Okanagan Mission today.

GHOST TOWNS

FAIRVIEW

Once the most renowned mining camp in the Okanagan. From 1892 to 1906 it was a wide open town - the metropolis of the south with a population of nearly 500 people. In those heady years there were dozens of business establishments scattered along the flats and far up the gulch. Half a dozen hotels catered to all types and there was a wide choice of hosteleries, ranging from Moffat's crude log cabin hotel to the elegant Hotel Fairview, also known as the "Big Teepee" and considered one of the finest stopping places in the entire interior.

For over a decade the mines in the gulch; the Morning Star, Brown Bear, Stemwinder and a myriad of others gave up their golden wealth and by the turn of the century Fairview was considered to be a town to be reckoned with. A dusty, sweltering place, it was the crossroads of the south Okanagan with stagecoach connections east to Camp McKinney, north to Penticton and south across the border to Oroville.

But tragedy dogged the town; first a diptheria epidemic, then a fire which razed the great Hotel Fairview and finally the shutdown of the mines when the ore began to play out. By 1907, Fairview was on its last legs and before another decade was out it was almost deserted. Within a few

The Hotel Fairview in 1899; known far and wide as the "Big Teepee." This impressive structure reigned over the town for three glorious years until it was completley gutted by fire in 1902. When it went - so did Fairview.

Stage Co a/c December 1899

7 To Barnie 2 meals Bed & Stall 1 45
8 To S Driver's meal 25
10 To S Drivers meals 25
12 To S Drivers Meal Hay 4 Horses 2 00
14 To S Drivers Meal Hay 4 Horses 1 00
13 Hay 4 Horses 2 00
15 To S Drivers Meal Hay 8 Horses [illegible] 2 meals Bed Dinner 5 80
16 To S Drivers Dinner 25
19 To S Drivers Dinner 25
21 To S Drivers Dinner 25
23 To S Drivers Dinner 25
26 To S Drivers Dinner Hay for Horses 1 00
27 To Hay 4 Horses 2 00
28 To Hay 3 Horses Stage Drivers Dinner 1 50
29 To Hay 4 Horses 2 00
31 [illegible] 2 meals Bed Stall 1 70
[illegible] 20 55
[illegible] 3 meals 3 25
4 20
[illegible] 78 05
Jan 1st To Balance 63 85
78 01

Stage Co. January 1900

4 To [illegible] 2 meals Bed Stall 1 70
Jan 5 By [illegible] 27 45
6 To [illegible] 2 meals Bed Stall 2 00
Jan 9 [illegible] 3 Meals Bed Stable Horse 2 00
9 Stage Drivers Dinner
Jan 11th [illegible] 3 Meals Bed Stable Horse 2 00
13 Stage Drivers Dinner
14th [illegible] McCrory Stable Horse 3 Meals Bed 2 00
15 [illegible] Stable Horses 3 Meals Bed 2 00
16 Stage Drivers Dinner
17 [illegible] Bed 1 70
Jan 27 [illegible] McCrory To Stable Horses [illegible] Bed Lunch 2 00
Jan 28 [illegible] To Stable Horses [illegible] Bed 2 00
Jan 31 [illegible] To Stable Horses 2 Meals Bed 1 70
By Bill of Jan 20th 12 62
By Bill Jan 26 35 12
Stage Driver To 13 meals 3 25 78 19
[illegible] 10 00
By [illegible] 32 35 45 84
To Balance Feb 1st 88.01

Meals for the stagecoach drivers were 25¢ in Fairview in 1900.

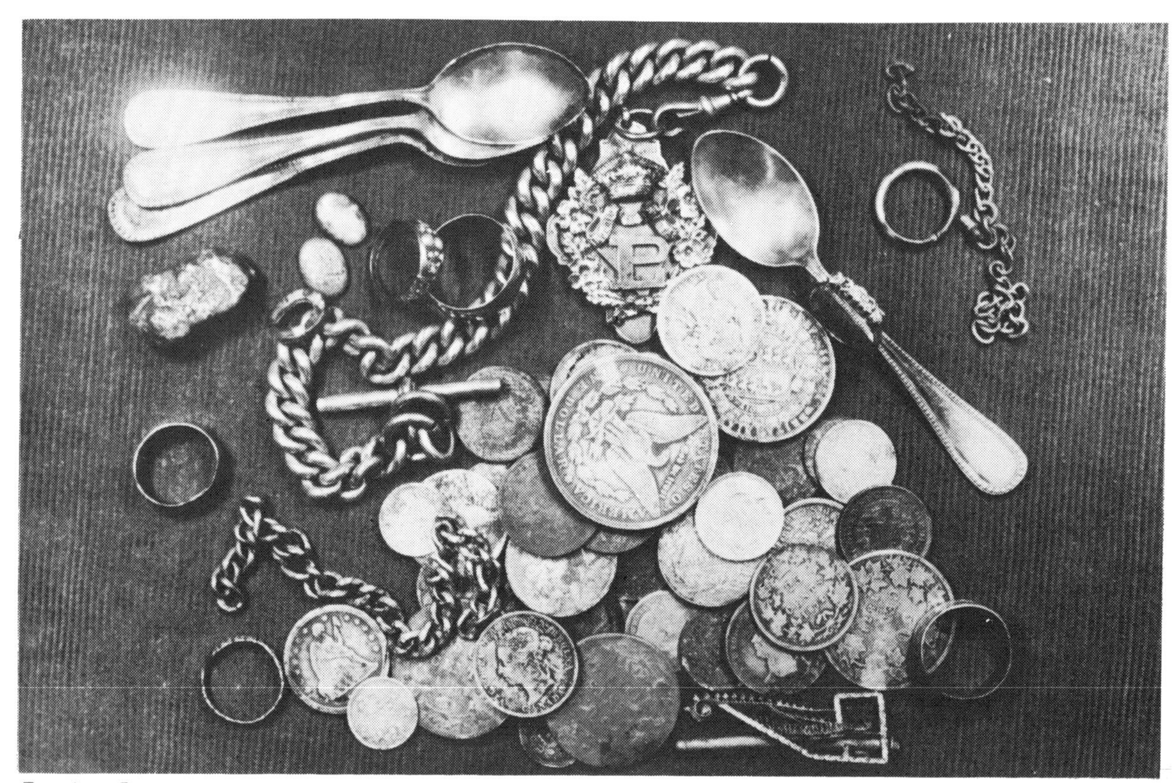

Part of a treasure trove recovered in Fairview in 1969 by the writer and associate, C. Murray. Shown are gold and silver items which include gold and diamond rings, gold and silver coins, gold jewellery, solid silver chains and miscellaneous other articles of precious metal.

FAIRVIEW TOWNSITE

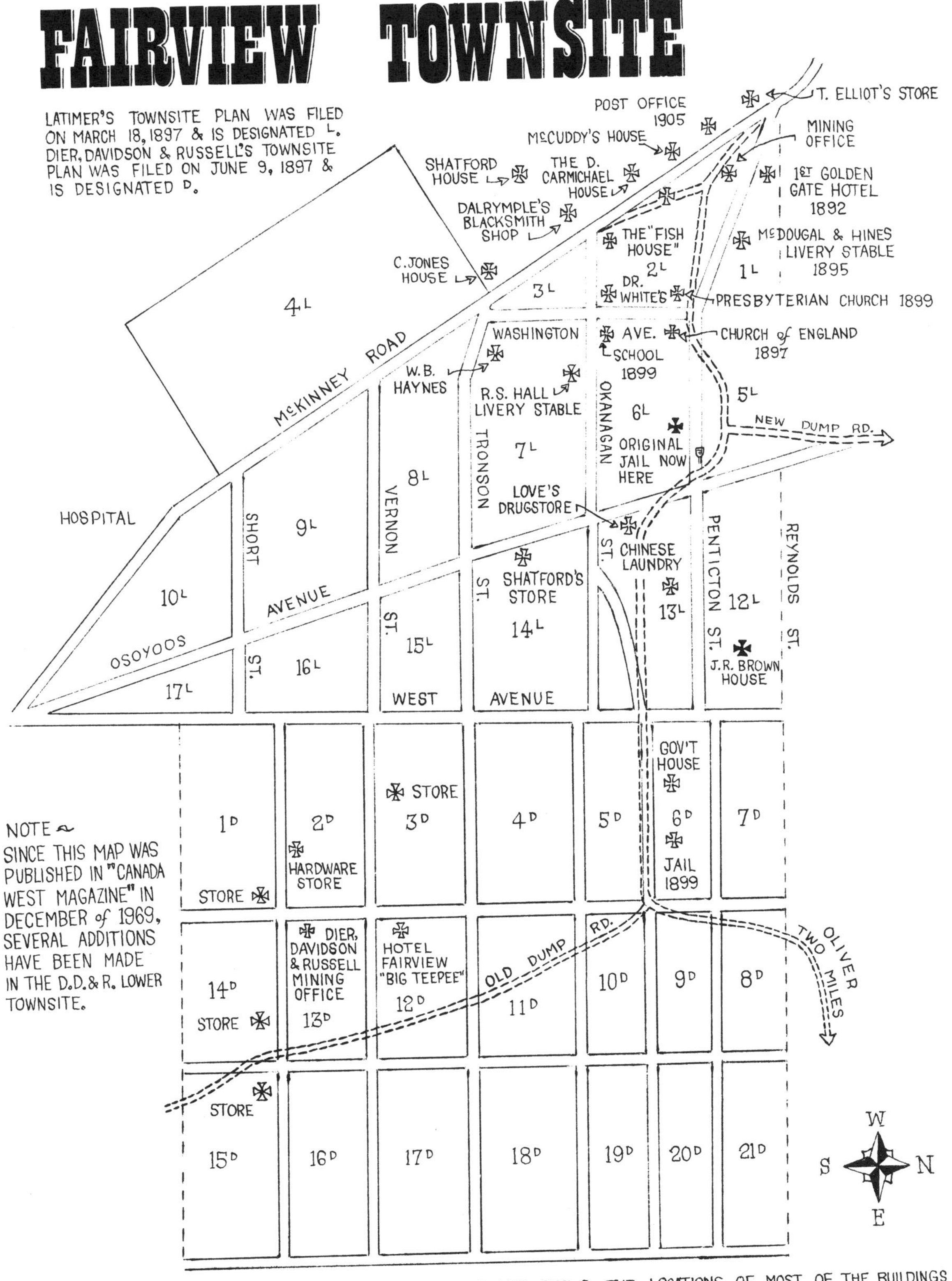

LEGEND

- ═══ PRESENT ROADS
- ✠ ORIGINAL BUILDING LOCATIONS
- ✚ ORIGINAL BUILDING STANDING
- 15L ORIGINAL TOWN LOTS

THIS MAP SHOWS THE LOCATIONS OF MOST OF THE BUILDINGS IN FAIRVIEW AFTER 1894. THERE WERE A NUMBER OF BUILDINGS PRIOR TO THAT DATE WHOSE EXACT LOCATIONS HAVE BEEN IMPOSSIBLE TO TRACE. NOT SHOWN ON THE MAP ARE THE BUILDINGS OUTSIDE THE LIMITS OF THE TOWNSITE SUCH AS THE GULCH SETTLEMENT, THE BLUE HOUSE, MOFFAT'S SALOON, THE MINER'S REST AND AN UNDETERMINED NUMBER OF OTHER BUILDINGS IN THE GENERAL AREA OF FAIRVIEW.

Still standing on the sagebrush covered flats - this is the Fairview jail.

The Fairview cemetery overlooking the south valley.

years fires and the inevitable salvagers had done their work and today only the hillside cemetery, the original jailhouse, Moffat's old log cabin saloon up the gulch and the overgrown foundations on the townsite mark its passing.

MINEOLA

Occasionally a community exists and never really leaves a mark and when it disappears it does so almost without a trace; its rise and fall going virtually unnoticed. Such a town was Mineola, a little known lumber town deep in the Okanagan hills. Once significant enough to warrent its own post office, it was a busy little camp for well over a decade.

No great catastrophe befell Mineola, it simply passed from view like innumerable lumber camps before it. Today few people even know its name and only a handful of coins, some blown bottles and an occasional rusty implement from the past attest to its existence.

THE OKANAGAN MISSION

The oldest white settlement still standing in the Okanagan valley. Founded by an Oblate missionary, Father Pandosy, in 1859, it was from this headquarters that the Oblates ranged through the Okanagan country carrying the cross to the Indians.

Today the mission stands restored, with many of the original log buildings, on its old site south of the city of Kelowna.

Part of the Okanagan Mission today.

O'KEEFE

This historic ranch was founded in 1867 by Cornelius O'Keefe, a cattleman who came to be called, "The O'Keefe of Okanagan." This capable Irishman built a cattle empire in the rolling hills nearby and his ranch; known as either O'Keefe or Okanagan, was the early center of trade.

Eventually, a Roman Catholic church, a general store and a post office became the main buildings in the settlement.

Today O'Keefe, which is still in possession of the original O'Keefe family, has been authentically restored with the old church and the ranch house as the nucleus of the restoration of the century old ranch.

O'Keefe today.

OLD CHERRYVILLE

Between 1876 and 1890, Old Cherryville was a placer gold camp located in a narrow draw along the banks of the south fork of Cherry Creek. At the height of its prominence, it probably numbered nearly 100 miners; both Chinese and White, who were either mining gold on the creek or seeking to located the lost silver lead close by.

Today, little remains of this old camp, although nearly a dozen log cabins in varying degrees of decay may still be seen along the creek (now called Monashee Creek) several miles east of the site of the present day Cherryville.

So, Old Cherryville, like all the placer camps of yesterday, has gone the way they have gone and only when a passerby happens across a piece of miner's equipment or a blown bottle from that other century, do visions of that past come briefly to life once again.

Some blown bottles and miscellaneous items from the original Cherryville placer gold camp. (Courtesy of the Heal Collection)

The remains of nearly a dozen log cabins may still be seen along the banks of Monashee Creek where the first Cherryville was located.

GOLD CREEKS

● Cherry Creek - Placer gold was reported in quantity on the south fork of this creek (the south fork is now known as Monashee Creek) in 1876. In the first years a great deal of coarse gold and some nuggets were found; the largest nugget weighing 8½ ounces with a gold value of $130 when gold was bringing $20 a pure ounce. In those early days; Christien, Schneider, Bissett, Leblanc and various other miners took out considerable amounts of placer gold from the 3½ miles of good paying ground which was located on Monashee Creek from its junction with Cherry and back upstream for that distance. This stream was worked rather extensively by both Chinese and white miners for fifteen years. The pay streak was from 4" above bedrock down to that layer. The placer gold is unusually high in silver with the result that the fineness is reputed to be the poorest in the province, usually running around .720 fine. Prospects: This stream must still be considered to be one of the best in the Okanagan region although it has been well worked. Still some possibilities for wing-damming although some was done in the discovery years, some of the benches also have potential.

● Harris Creek - This stream is situated to the south of the village of Lumby in the North Okanagan. A small creek which has yielded coarse gold and some good nuggets. Although the entire output of the creek has amounted to approximately $125,000; some operators have done extremely well on the

Monashee Creek today.

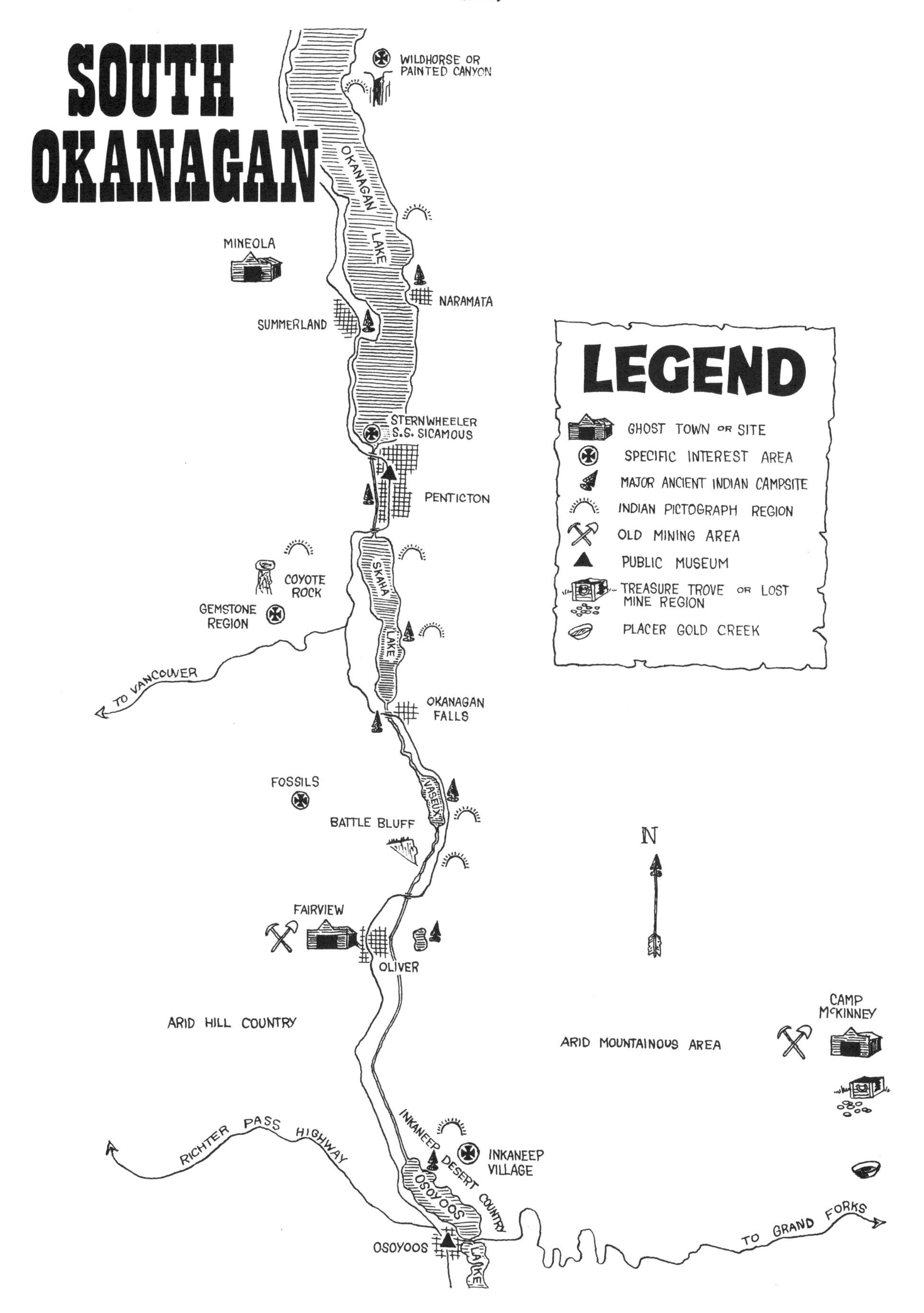
SOUTH OKANAGAN
WILDHORSE OR PAINTED CANYON
OKANAGAN LAKE
MINEOLA
NARAMATA
SUMMERLAND
STERNWHEELER S.S. SICAMOUS
PENTICTON
LEGEND
GHOST TOWN OR SITE
SPECIFIC INTEREST AREA
MAJOR ANCIENT INDIAN CAMPSITE
INDIAN PICTOGRAPH REGION
OLD MINING AREA
PUBLIC MUSEUM
TREASURE TROVE OR LOST MINE REGION
PLACER GOLD CREEK
COYOTE ROCK
GEMSTONE REGION
SKAHA LAKE
TO VANCOUVER
OKANAGAN FALLS
FOSSILS
VASEUX
BATTLE BLUFF
N
FAIRVIEW
OLIVER
ARID HILL COUNTRY
ARID MOUNTAINOUS AREA
CAMP McKINNEY
RICHTER PASS HIGHWAY
INKANEEP DESERT COUNTRY
INKANEEP VILLAGE
OSOYOOS
OSOYOOS LAKE
TO GRAND FORKS

relatively short length of good ground. Prospects: Most of the best parts of Harris are held and there are few possibilities left for the prospector who is not already established on this creek. The gold is high in purity on this creek which will probably continue to yield gold for some time to come.

Looking north on Mission Creek. This photograph shows the part of the valley below the canyon where most of the placer gold was recovered.

● Lambly Creek - Called Bear Creek locally. In 1876, placer gold was discovered on this stream which empties into Okanagan Lake from the west across from Kelowna. Although a few nuggets up to $5 value have been recovered on this creek, the gold tends to be fine with the best pay ground above the falls. Prospects: Rather limited although thorough prospecting of the lower benches might prove up something worthwhile. It would, however, be unwise to expect much from a creek which even in its heyday was only considered to be "so-so."

● Mission Creek - Known as a placer creek in 1876 but probably discovered a year or two earlier. Originally known as Riviere L'Anse du Sable, this creek is south of Kelowna and empties into Okanagan Lake from the eastern hills. The best ground was found approximately seven miles from its mouth and thereon up to the canyon a short distance above. Virtually no gold was recovered above the canyon which has led to speculation that an ancient high channel lies to the north-west. The gold was generally fine with a few nuggets above the one pennyweight size. In the 1870's, good claims - like McDougall's, were yielding only 5 pennyweight per hand. Prospects :

An early hydraulic operation on Nashwito (Siwash) Creek which flows into Okanagan Lake south of Vernon. Placer gold was discovered on this stream in the 1870's.

Lambly (Bear) Creek in the Okanagan across the lake from Kelowna. One of several gold bearing streams on the west side of Okanagan Lake.

not especially promising although drifting could prove worthwhile. In the early years some snipers made a fairly good living. The last of the old prospectors, Dan Gallagher, eked out a living on the creek until the 1940's.

A ruined bridge over Mission Creek near the old placer workings.

● Nashwito Creek - A gold placer creek which is still known by its old name, Siwash. Over the years a considerable amount of work has been done along this stream; tunneling to bed-rock in the discovery years, ground-sluicing and some hydraulicking later. The benches have also produced a reasonable amount of gold with the best ground lying about 2 miles above the mouth of the stream which flows into Okanagan Lake from the west, a few miles south of Vernon. Prospects: some possibilities although the best ground has already been worked fairly extensively.

● Shuswap River - Although not noted as a placer river, gold has been recovered from time to time along stretches of the Shuswap in interesting quantity. The most productive area lies below Sugar Lake with the gold being usually fine, unlike the gold from either Cherry (Monashee) or Harris Creeks in the same region. Prospects: there are more likely placer rivers and creeks than the Shuswap which must be considered marginal at best.

● Whiteman Creek - This creek flows into Okanagan Lake from the west and was reputedly discovered in the 1870's. Some placer gold was taken out of this stream, especially prior to 1922. In recent years, however, there has been little worthwhile activity on this creek. Prospects: not exceptional mainly because the gold recovered was generally fine and not in any large quantity. Its history is not encouraging.

INDIAN COUNTRY

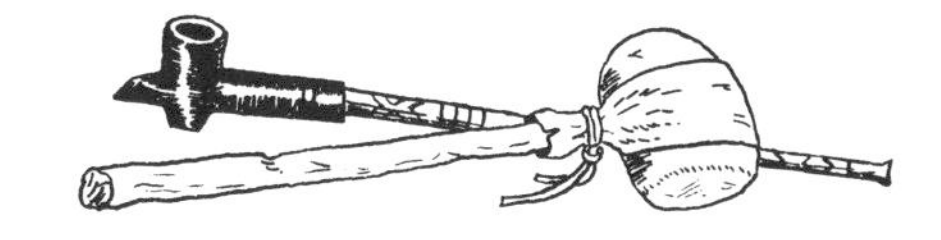

A wide valley and a chain of lakes. Redfish, salmon, big game and waterfowl in abundance. This was the Okanagan the Indians knew more than a century ago.

Before the arrival of the fur men, it has been estimated that there were 1,200 Okanagans of the great Salishan nation in the main valley and no fewer than twenty villages of major importance.

In the arid south country from Osoyoos to Oliver, James A. Teit, the noted authority, mentioned two major camps: one was the village known as Soi'yus, which meant "meeting," and undoubtedly referred to that narrow spit of land which cuts Osoyoos Lake. This camp was located on the west side of the lake and is now within the limits of the town of Osoyoos, it was abandoned somewhere around 1855 and a number of fine artifacts and a representative collection of burial items have been found on this ancient site.

Many of the natural camping places along the shores of Osoyoos Lake were also used from time to time by the Okanagans. One of them, Nkami'p, which meant "at the base or bottom," was a significant camp on the east side near the mouth of Inkaneep Creek. Even now, the Indians frequent this same area and although the Indian Reserve encompasses most of the east side of the lake, they live in picturesque Inkaneep Village in the back

The Inkaneep desert country near Osoyoos Lake.

"Buffalo Man" Rock near the old Indian horse trail in Inkaneep. There are a number of Indian pictographs painted on the face of this rock.

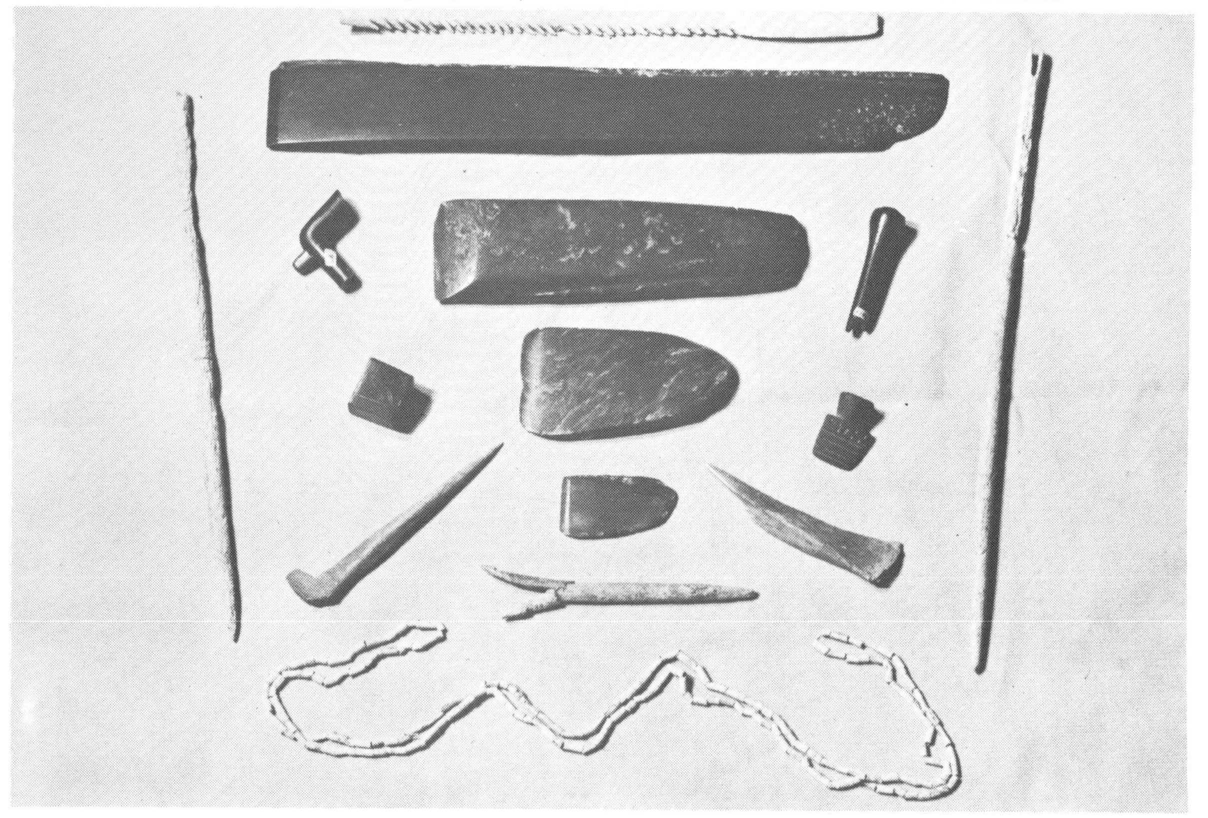

Some Okanagan Indian artifacts from the Penticton Museum Collection.

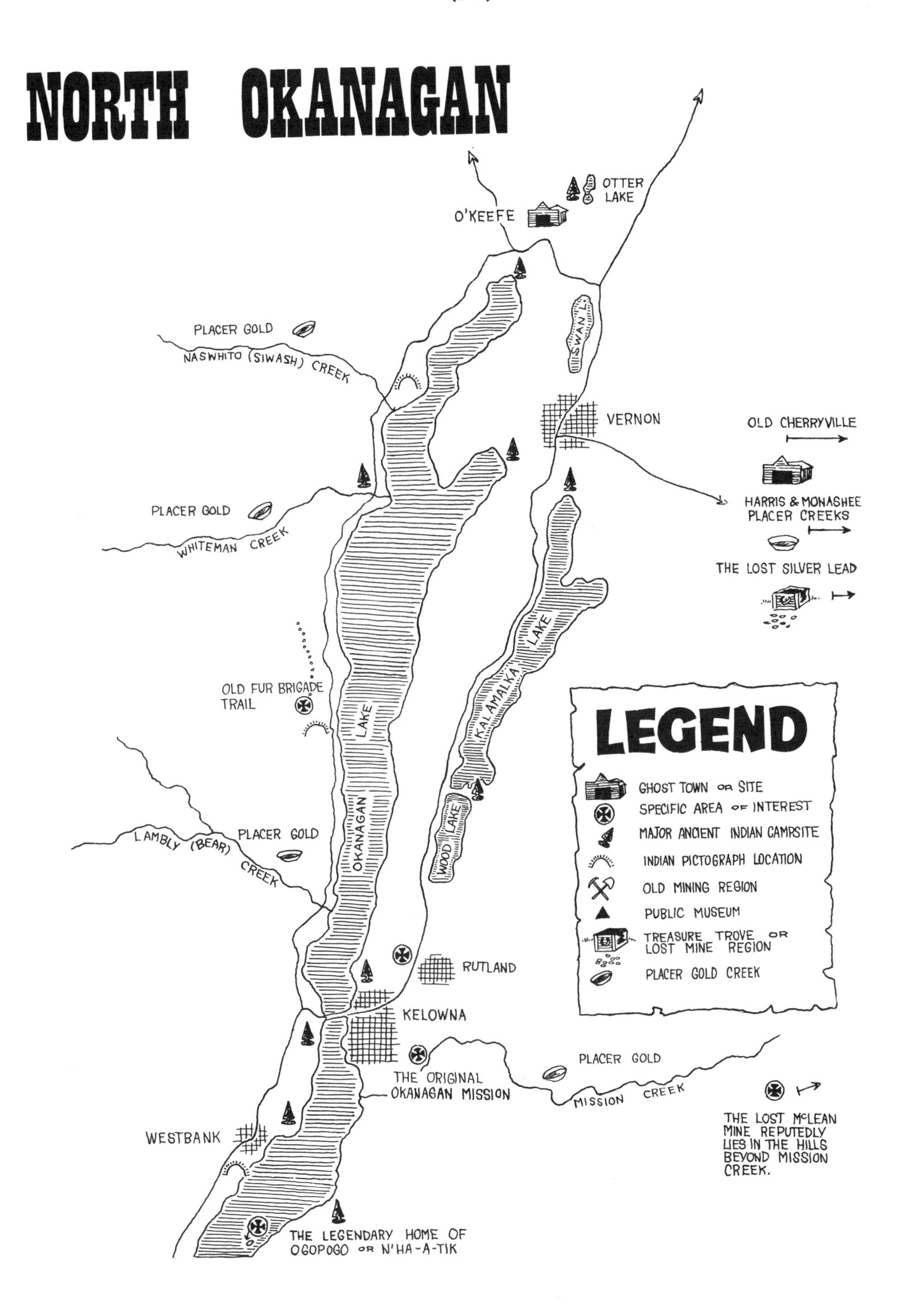
NORTH OKANAGAN
OTTER LAKE
O'KEEFE
PLACER GOLD
NASWHITO (SIWASH) CREEK
SWAN L.
VERNON
OLD CHERRYVILLE
PLACER GOLD
WHITEMAN CREEK
HARRIS & MONASHEE PLACER CREEKS
THE LOST SILVER LEAD
OLD FUR BRIGADE TRAIL
KALAMALKA LAKE
OKANAGAN LAKE
WOOD LAKE
PLACER GOLD
LAMBLY (BEAR) CREEK
LEGEND
GHOST TOWN OR SITE
SPECIFIC AREA OF INTEREST
MAJOR ANCIENT INDIAN CAMPSITE
INDIAN PICTOGRAPH LOCATION
OLD MINING REGION
PUBLIC MUSEUM
TREASURE TROVE OR LOST MINE REGION
PLACER GOLD CREEK
RUTLAND
KELOWNA
PLACER GOLD
THE ORIGINAL OKANAGAN MISSION
MISSION CREEK
THE LOST McLEAN MINE REPUTEDLY LIES IN THE HILLS BEYOND MISSION CREEK.
WESTBANK
THE LEGENDARY HOME OF OGOPOGO OR N'HA-A-TIK

country, several miles up this old favourite fishing stream, preferring it to the lakeshore. Indeed, this lonely desert land on the east side of the lake is indelible - unlike any other part of the Okanagan.

The Indian trails swing northward, past Oliver and Tugulnuit Lake; another camping ground of yesteryear, on up the valley past looming Battle Bluff and the lake called Vaseux, where the Okanagans tarried on their way to the fishing grounds at Okanagan Falls.

At the falls in those days, the Indians had a year-round village, for it was one of the choicest fishing spots in the whole interior. Before the present dam was constructed, there was a series of rapids and falls through which the redfish and salmon had to pass to reach their spawning grounds and it was here that the Indians congregated in great numbers to spear the fish. The main village here was called Sxoxene'tk, although a dozen lesser camps also graced the immediate vicinity.

The Indian trail split to both sides of Skaha Lake, past pictograph sites and on to the big village called Penti'kten, halfway between the Big Lake and Skaha - although the old Indian camp has been abandoned for almost a century now, it covered nearly twenty acres at one time and has yielded some of the most perfectly chipped arrowpoints and knives found in the valley.

On the Big Lake, or Okanagan as we now know it, the main trail went along the benches of the east side, through majestic Painted or Wildhorse Canyon and north to the village of Skela'un.na, or "grizzly bear place," which we know by the more lyrical name Kelowna.

Deep in the Marron valley of the south Okanagan is "Coyote Rock," which was supposedly Chief Coyote's boundary marker. The legends of the Okanagan Indians attribute mystical powers to it.

Some Okanagan Indian artifacts from the Canada West Collection.

An ancient Indian village called Sxoxene'tk, meaning "swift rough water place," once stood on the flats to the right. The Okanagans congregated at this spot each autumn to spear the redfish and salmon on their runs.

At this widest part of the valley, several important villages stood; Stekatkolxne'ut, a village on the lakeshore below Westbank, and slightly to the north, Stekatelxene'ut, another village on the west side of the lake situated on a sandy point which is now covered by the approach to the Okanagan Lake bridge.

All along the Big Lake, at the mouths of most creeks and at other logical places were either temporary or permanent campsites. Near the head of the lake was Nkama'peleks meaning "neck end," and farther to the north stood Sntlemuxte'n or "place where slaughtered," probably a reference to a now forgotten battle of the past. North of Okanagan Lake, on a little lake known as Otter, was Tse'ketku, the main fishing camp in the north.

But the villages were not confined strictly to the valley proper: places like Nkekema'peleks, Tselo'tsus and Tsxelho'qem, all important villages at one time were found on the shores of Kalamalka Lake and there were scores of smaller base camps in gathering and hunting regions all through the Okanagan.

Although that era has vanished as has that artistic generation, their legacy can still be found along the back trails - a vivid Indian painting on a cliff face, a beautifully chipped arrowhead in the dust or the still discernible kekuli depressions in a vacated Indian village - reminders of the years when the Okanagan was truly "Indian Country."

Majestic McIntyre or Battle Bluff in the Vaseux Lake country. Many years ago, according to the Indians, a great battle was fought on the very edge of this bluff between the Okanagans and the Shuswaps. Okanagan Indians to this day do not trespass on the "haunted ground" at the top of the cliff.

TREASURE TROVE

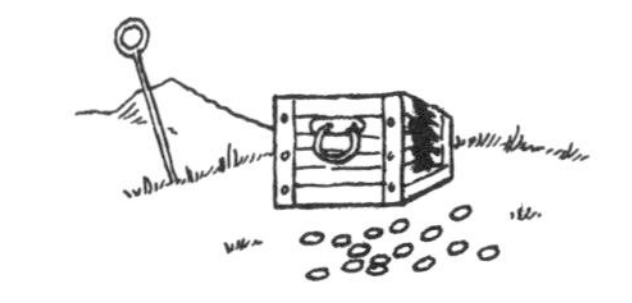

THE LOST SILVER LEAD

In the early 1870's, prospectors discovered an outcrop of silver ore on the south side of Monashee Creek in the Old Cherryville region. The ore from this outcrop proved to be so rich that it assayed out at more than $1,500.00 a ton. This fabulous vein was followed and some shipments were made before it mysteriously narrowed and finally petered out.

The lead, however, was located again several years later and more of the ore sacked and shipped. The ore was astonishing because many of the samples were almost pure silver. But again the lead pinched out and once more frantic attempts were made by a number of mining companies to re-locate it. Some miners, like Donald McIntyre and L.W. Riske, persevered for almost twenty years in their efforts to strike the vein but they and others since then were all finally forced to admit defeat.

It has been speculated that this vein may be the mother lode of the placer gold in the creek because the silver content in the placer gold is higher than in any other creek in British Columbia and they contend that the vein may change its character to a predominantly gold vein farther to the east and upstream.

So the Lost Silver Lead still waits to be re-discovered in a steep draw of Monashee Creek near Old Cherryville.

The old workings by Monashee Creek near the "Lost Silver Lead."

Bound for booming Greenwood, the Bassett Brothers freighting outfits pass through the rival town of Anaconda, B.C. - circa 1899.

THE BOUNDARY COUNTRY

INTRODUCTION

The Boundary Country - shoulder to shoulder with history, from the high hill country of old Camp McKinney, east to the mountain lake they call Christina. This is the land where historic mining trails pass by a dozen towns of yesterday; Rock Creek, Boundary Falls, Anaconda, Phoenix, Cascade and other towns whose names still ring out from the past.

A country where the Kettle river still winds lazily through the length of the region, where the Salish Indians traversed only the open country and the horse trails, and where the solitude of the North Fork and the Head of the Lake is unsurpassed.

Here, the mind's eye can still almost see the miners tramping into the gold creeks like Rock and Boundary and driving in claim stakes in the hard-rock country; envisioning another million dollar mine like Highland-Bell or Old Ironsides. And the call from the past is still strong in this Boundary Country - the land of the Dewdney Trail.

An abandoned hotel in Westbridge.

GHOST TOWNS

ANACONDA

Once a formidable rival of Greenwood, Anaconda lay a mile west of the former on an attractive flat - ideal for a townsite, and in the boom years this advantage was loudly mooted by its supporters. By 1896, half a dozen businesses had established on its one main street. By the following year, however, Greenwood had gained the upper hand and slowly Anaconda slipped into obscurity and within a decade had all but disappeared.

Today, only a few log structures and the faint outlines of a city street are all that remain to mark its passing.

BOUNDARY FALLS

The site of this old camp is barely recognizable now although it, like many other mining camps in the area, was touted as the coming center in the late 1890's. Close by are found the falls on Boundary Creek from which the town derived its name.

In 1902, the famous Sunset smelter was blown in and with innumerable promising claims close by the future seemed secure, but when the price of copper plummeted after 1918, the smelter was forced to close and when it shut down so did Boundary Falls.

Now only the great slag heaps by the banks of the creek and the long overgrown foundations on the townsite can be seen by the passerby.

The Dominion Copper Company's smelter at Boundary Falls, B.C. This was the economic mainstay of the mining camp and its fortunes ebbed when the smelter closed.

CAMP McKINNEY

In 1887 one of the earliest lode gold camps in the province was born. It was named Camp McKinney after one of the four original prospectors who had staked claims in the area. By 1893, the camp was roaring on the strength of excellent assays from claims like the Cariboo, Amelia, Alice, Emma and Okanagan. The former two later developed into the premier mine of the camp; the renowned Cariboo-Amelia which held the distinction of being the first lode mine in the province to pay dividends. For a full decade the mining camp ran full tilt with shipments of gold bullion being made regularly.

By 1901, probably the peak year for McKinney, the population stood at 250 and along its main street hotels like the St. Louis, Sailor, Camp McKinney, McBoyle & West's, Cariboo and Miner's Exchange competed for the miners trade. In from the west clattered the stages of the Hall Line from Fairview and from the east came Meyerhoff's stage from Midway, and the Okanagan Indians from Inkameep mixed with rough whites from all corners of North America. The business section became almost cosmopolitan with three general stores, a drug store, a real estate office, a butcher shop, a school and a church counted among the amenities of the camp.

By 1904, however, the inevitable happened. Values decreased at the 600 foot level and operations at the Cariboo Mine were terminated.

When the illustrious Cariboo closed, the camp went downhill rapidly and within months it was nearly a ghost town. Although there were several

Log hotel at Camp McKinney in 1895. This was probably the Cariboo Hotel, one of six in the old mining camp prior to the turn of the century.

Camp McKinney's main street in the late 1890's.

Some of the miners in front of the Little Cariboo bunkhouse in McKinney Camp - circa 1898.

attempts from 1907 on to revive the camp, they never really succeeded and it never again approached its previous prominence.

Although the total gold output of the camp amounted to 81,000 ounces and it was acclaimed as an important lode camp in its day, little remains of the camp itself for in 1919 and again in 1931 devastating forest fires swept through the region destroying virtually the entire town.

Now only the cemetery and a few abandoned workings indicate the site and of the few trespassers on this mountain hideaway most are treasure hunters who haunt the vicinity and the hills nearby searching vainly for Matt Roderick's lost gold bars.

The hotel called the Smith House in deserted Carmi.

CARMI

Carmi came onto the scene just after the turn of the century; founded on the strength of a hectic mineral rush to the area and faith in the Carmi silver mine in the hills nearby. By 1910, "Trapper" Smith's hotel and a collection of crude log and frame houses gave it the right to be called a town.

But the Carmi mine, unlike the great Highland-Bell in neighbouring Beaverdell, was short-lived and when it finally ceased operations Carmi was doomed. The town hung on through three more precarious decades until the last of the die-hards left and the town was abandoned.

Today, the quaint old Smith House waits forlornly for another rush that will never come-for Carmi is a forgotten town.

CASCADE CITY

"Fair city of Cascade - the gem of the west
Whom nature designed as the grandest - the best..."

This glowing tribute to Cascade was printed in an 1898 issue of the CASCADE RECORD. In that year, with the Boundary Country literally jumping with mining activity, nearly all the supplies from Spokane and other points in the United States were routed through Cascade and it soon became known as "The Gateway City." At the time it seemed that the town couldn't miss; the Canadian Pacific Railway had announced plans to build a smelter on the edge of the townsite and the town itself was ideally laid out and well located with coming rail connections, water power and mining claims close by.

All through that year there was feverish activity as Cascade grew in importance. Down on First Avenue, hotels like the Cascade, Club, Scandia, Cosmopolitan, Montana, Grand Central and half a dozen others catered to the needs of the travel-weary who were given a wide choice; fine liquors, stud poker, blackjack or even feminine company of somewhat questionable profession. Up on Main Street other business establishments; watchmaker, bakery, pharmacy, cafes and even a shoe shop could be found. Thus, it was

In 1898, the jail contract was let and the Cascade jail, a structure 20 x 30 feet in size and containing three cells, was built on the flats some distance from town at a cost of $445. This photograph, taken in 1969, shows the remains of the old jail with two handmade, square bars and the bar of the original jail door in the foreground.

Freighting teams along First Avenue in Cascade City in 1898.

Cascade City in the summer of 1899. On the left is First Avenue and in the right background is Main Street. Population 1,000.

little wonder that the Dec. 17, 1898, issue of the RECORD contained the headline - "Eve of Prosperity."

Unknown to the residents of the city, however, the die had been cast earlier in the year when the boy millionaire, F. Augustus Heinze sold his Trail Creek Landing holdings, including his smelter, to the C.P.R. Although the railroad company continued to insist that it was going ahead with its Cascade smelter, it became increasingly obvious when months went by without activity that the proposed smelter would never be built. This unexpected blow, coupled with the failure to develop any worthwhile mineral claims in the immediate area, caused the stock of the town to plummet.

On Sept. 30, 1899, when ten buildings on First Avenue were destroyed in a flash fire, it was indicative that the town had slipped and when, early in 1901, another fire, probably of incendiary origin, nearly wiped out the rest of First Avenue, Cascade was beyond redemption. By 1903, no more 75 inhabitants remained of the 1,000 three years before.

Although a few persistent souls like R.G. Ritchie stayed on in the town for another 45 years, it never recovered and by 1950 it was less than a ghost town as a result of sporadic fires down through the years.

Today, the townsite is almost unrecognizeable; a few foundations, a depression here and there - not much left of Cascade City.

The site of Gladstone City in 1970.

CORYELL OR GLADSTONE

Back in the underbrush, near a little creek called McRae Creek, are the remains of Gladstone City.

Today it is called Coryell but in 1898 it was Gladstone - a boom town which claimed three hotels, an equal number of stores, a livery stable and several other short-lived enterprises.

Gladstone came into being on the strength of railroading and mining; for the many surface outcrops in Burnt Basin indicated gold, silver and copper in exciting quantity. For months the town lunged ahead and hotels like the Gladstone and Ennis and Flynns kept open twenty-four hours each day to accommodate the influx of prospectors and mining men who flocked into the area to examine Burnt Basin.

Alas, the properties in Burnt Basin proved exciting on the surface only and within weeks Gladstone, which had pinned its hopes on a mining future, was being vacated. By 1899, businesses which had been looked upon as going concerns a few months before, were being advertised at a fraction of their original cost and even then there were no takers. So, Gladstone City is no more and the ever encroaching underbrush has masked the site where it once stood. Today, only a sign by the highway with the single word "Coryell" denotes its existence.

The Algoma Hotel in Deadwood in 1933. This was one of the two hotels in this little-known mining town in the Boundary Country.

DEADWOOD CAMP

On Webster Brown's 1897 map of the Boundary is the name Deadwood. In that era, several miles west of Greenwood, a number of copper claims like the Big Ledge, Eagle, Butte City, Spoiled Horse and Mother Lode gave rise to this mining camp. The Mother Lode was destined to become a great mine but the town it spawned was fated to disappear within a few years.

Strangely, Deadwood Camp never really left its mark although it once contained two hotels, a store, a post office and even a school. You won't see much on the flats today, even the traces of the Algoma Hotel, which survived for years after the decline of the camp, have virtually disappeared - Deadwood is just what the name implies.

EHOLT

A unique name for an odd town. Although various explanations have been advanced concerning the origin of the name, it was actually named after one Louis Eholt who pre-empted two lots on a small creek east of Greenwood and by 1893, the stopping-place of Eholt and Eholt Creek came into being.

Six years later, the Columbia and Western Railway came through Eholt and in that same year a post office was established. With the coming of the railroad the little village surged ahead and by 1900 it laid claim to five hotels: the Kaiser, Summit, Columbia, Eholt and Northern. It also had four stores, a blacksmith, a doctor and a "Mining Exchange" office,

Eholt around 1910.

The C.P.R. yards at Eholt in the busy years.

The Hotel Northern and other business buildings in Eholt - circa 1900.

and the population stood at a respectable 250.

With the western Boundary country humming with mining activity, the town became the divisional point for the C.P.R. when it bought out the Columbia and Western. That made the town.

With the prolific mines at nearby Phoenix running full blast, as many as fifteen locomotives and crews operated out of the little town to keep the copper ore moving to the smelters at Grand Forks and Greenwood.

Those were the days of colourful engineers like "Wild Bill" Harriott, Harry Shrapnell, "Happy" McPherson and a host of other railroad men who highballed out of Eholt. But Eholt's existence depended solely on Phoenix, and when the Granby Company was finally forced to terminate operations in Phoenix in 1919 due to falling copper prices, both places were hard hit. Phoenix rapidly became a ghost town and Eholt's population began to drift to other places. By 1939, only 50 people remained and when the post office closed a few years later, Eholt officially came to an end.

Now it's just another name in passing - trees growing in the middle of the old main street, hundreds of broken bottles and the barely visible remains of fallen buildings scattered along the townsite. The town once called Eholt is not even recognizeable today.

GREENWOOD

Greenwood, like so many of the Boundary towns, got its start because of mining. In 1886, several mineral claims had been recorded in a narrow gulch nearly ten miles north of the mouth of Boundary Creek. When the ore samples assayed high in copper, rumours began to circulate about the rich

The city of Greenwood as it appeared in 1900.

showings in the area and more prospectors drifted in. A decade later, the number of claims had increased many times and the surrounding area gave indications of great promise.

One of the first individuals who foresaw the possibilities of a camp arising from the activities was a merchant from the Okanagan, one Robert Wood. By 1895, he had erected a log store and named the surrounding region "Greenwood." By the next year there were three hotels, a livery stable, a first-rate general store, two assay offices, a mining broker and a dozen other assorted establishments including an ill-fated opera house.

With new discoveries being reported regularly, Greenwood was clearly on the rise and by 1897 it became an incorporated city. Two years later, the town's population had climbed to 3,000 and its crowded main street, appropriately called Copper Street, was impressively ostentatious. It was in that same year that the tracks of the new Columbia and Western Railway finally reached Greenwood from the east and the coming of the railroad confirmed the importance of the center. Even fire, that dreaded bane of mining towns everywhere, didn't slow its ascent although both the Claredon and International Hotels as well as several other businesses were gutted by two conflagrations which struck in 1899.

1900 came and went and the city continued to prosper. When the Granby Company built a huge smelter at rival Grand Forks to handle the mountains of ore from Phoenix; Greenwood countered with a smelter of her own the following year when the first furnace of the B.C. Copper Company's plant was blown in to treat the ore from the famous Mother Lode mine. By 1902, a third smelter started operations three miles down Boundary Creek - a

The owners posing in front of the Elkhorn Brewery in Greenwood in 1899.

Visiting political dignitaries of the day are given the once-over by the miners standing along Copper Street in Greenwood. Circa 1899.

total of three smelters in the Boundary Country to handle the seemingly inexhaustible supply of ore from the camps near Greenwood. And would-be rival like Anaconda and Boundary Falls were never able to challenge the position of Greenwood as the supply center for the surrounding camps like Providence, Copper, Deadwood, Wellington, Central, Skylark and others.

As befitting its stature, the city became the seat of government for the Boundary and at one time nearly one hundred firms could be counted in its business district. Like all "big" mining towns, it had its own paper, first the "TIMES" and then in 1906, the "GREENWOOD LEDGE," which rapidly became required reading for mining men.

By 1910, although the boom years had passed, Greenwood's population stabilized at 1,500 and it, along with Phoenix, were considered to be the only two cities of any significance in the western Boundary.

For nearly a quarter of a century copper was the economic mainstay of the town and its prosperity depended on the well-being of that metal. In 1918, however, the bottom suddenly dropped out of the copper market; the results were immediate and ruinous and before the year was out, both the Greenwood and Boundary Falls smelters were idled and by the following year, even the great Granby smelter at Grand Forks had shut down. With no market and no smelters, the copper mines in the camps nearby also closed down. Eholt, Boundary Falls, Deadwood and even mighty Phoenix simply disappeared but Greenwood managed to survive.

Over half a century has passed since then and Greenwood, still an incorporated city, has changed but the visual evidence of the mining era may still be seen; the old courthouse with its impressive courtroom where

The remains of the B.C. Copper Company's smelter in Greenwood today.

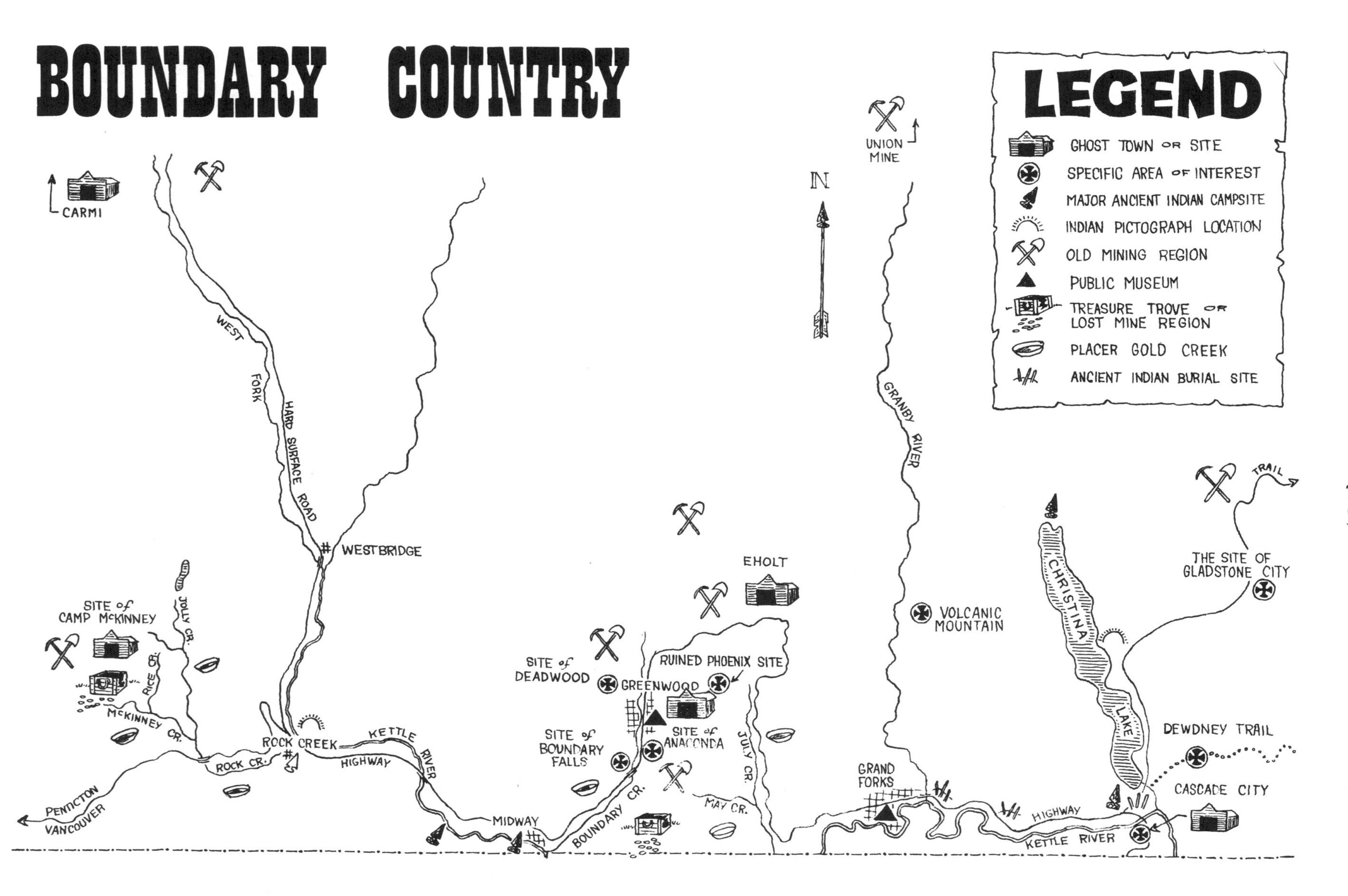
BOUNDARY COUNTRY
LEGEND
GHOST TOWN OR SITE
SPECIFIC AREA OF INTEREST
MAJOR ANCIENT INDIAN CAMPSITE
INDIAN PICTOGRAPH LOCATION
OLD MINING REGION
PUBLIC MUSEUM
TREASURE TROVE OR LOST MINE REGION
PLACER GOLD CREEK
ANCIENT INDIAN BURIAL SITE
CARMI
UNION MINE
N
WEST FORK
HARD SURFACE ROAD
WESTBRIDGE
GRANBY RIVER
TRAIL
THE SITE OF GLADSTONE CITY
CHRISTINA LAKE
VOLCANIC MOUNTAIN
EHOLT
SITE of CAMP McKINNEY
JOLLY CR.
RICE CR.
McKINNEY CR.
ROCK CR.
ROCK CREEK
KETTLE RIVER
HIGHWAY
SITE of DEADWOOD
GREENWOOD
RUINED PHOENIX SITE
SITE of BOUNDARY FALLS
SITE of ANACONDA
JULY CR.
MAY CR.
BOUNDARY CR.
MIDWAY
GRAND FORKS
DEWDNEY TRAIL
CASCADE CITY
PENTICTON
VANCOUVER
WASHINGTON STATE

the Supreme Court of Canada once sat in session is almost unchanged since that day, the remains of the B.C. Copper Company's smelter lie abandoned across Boundary Creek and the gaunt skeletons of mines like the Providence stand yet on the outskirts of this historic mining town.

PHOENIX

It was once "the highest incorporated city in Canada," and from its opulent mines, in a brief twenty years, flowed more wealth than all the gold in the Yukon produced. Today, not only Phoenix but even the original site have vanished completely, buried under thousands of tons of country rock. Strangely, the company chiefly responsible for its birth also presided at its death.

In the summer of 1891, two prospectors; Matt Hotter and Henry White, made their way up a precipitous draw, following an unnamed creek east of Greenwood. As they approached the 4,500 foot level they began to notice outcrops of obviously rich ore. After carefully picking their ground they located two claims which they named Old Ironsides and Knob Hill; both of which were later to become the nucleus of a gigantic copper operation. Soon after, the Brooklyn and Stemwinder properties were staked and then in rapid succession, other claims like the Gold Drop, Snowshoe, Rawhide, Victoria and dozens of others which were to add to this copper bonanza. By 1896, the realization that it was a magnificent ore body dawned, and the camp known as Greenwood Camp at that time, turned into a town. Three

The Knob Hill and Old Ironsides Mines when Phoenix was young.

Phoenix in her better years; a swank business district, boardwalks, fine hotels and most of the amenities of a city.

years later, in 1899, the city of Phoenix was incorporated.

And what a city it was, unique even in the annals of the Boundary Country: over two dozen hotels and saloons, churches, a school, brewery, jail, a newspaper called the PHOENIX PIONEER and scores of other thriving businesses. Down its boardwalks strode miners, promoters, prospectors, gamblers, riff-raff and not a few ladies of easy virtue. Hotels like the Union, Imperial, Victoria House, Maple Leaf, Queen's, Golden and others never closed their doors and high stake games and fine liquors were the order of the day. At the plush Brooklyn Hotel the cuisine was comparable to that of any other house in the entire west. Only in Phoenix would a judge like the legendary "Willie" Williams, dare to ride his horse through the swinging doors of a packed saloon to join the gambling fraternity in a no-holds-barred game of stud poker and where its hockey team was confident enough to challenge for the Stanley Cup, emblematic of world hockey supremacy. It was a roaring town for more than twenty years and in that space of time, the two railroads coming into the city; the V.V. & E. and the C.P.R., ran their ore trains twenty-four hours a day, seven days a week, carrying over 13,000,000 tons of ore to the smelters nearby.

But when the end came it came unexpectedly. In 1919, a strike of the coal miners in the East Kootenay paralyzed the town when the coal supply was cut off and when the price of copper dropped almost simultaneously, Phoenix was no longer economically viable. The Granby Consolidated shut

On the hill above the town, the mines lie deserted - 1919.

A few items from Phoenix - a swinging door from the Brooklyn Hotel, a fine keg from the brewery and several bottles. Surprisingly, a number of rare embossed H.B.Co. bottles were recovered from Phoenix.

down its smelter in Grand Forks that same year and operations at the mines ground to a halt. In 1919, Phoenix had been a city, by 1920, it was a ghost town and completely deserted; the inhabitants had simply walked away and in many instances had not even bothered to take their personal effects with them - houses were left complete with original furniture and saloons with mirrors, bars, spitoons, pianos and other furnishings intact.

Soon the salvage crews began to move in to dismantle the buildings and slowly Phoenix vanished. Thirty years later, little remained on the original site to indicate that a city had once existed there. Today, the Granby Company is back at the scene of its former triumphs and now even the townsite has been inundated by their open pit operations and only the overgrown cemetery in a draw below has escaped.

So, Phoenix of old has disappeared and with it has gone much of the grandeur of the era it presided over.

VOLCANIC CITY

Although articles have been written about Volcanic City, it never really existed except in the fertile imagination of "Volcanic Brown," a prospector who was undoubtedly one of the most colourful characters ever to set foot in the Boundary Country.

Before the turn of the century, Brown discovered a magnificent looking "iron cap" mountain up the North Fork of the Kettle River and he became convinced that it was "rich beyond compare." At the time he boasted that "all the lead pencils in Grand Forks can't total up its value." and swore that when his Volcanic Mine came into production, a different type of city would arise; one without any schools, churches or banks and which would be served by railroads coming in from the four cardinal directions. Alas, Brown's dream never materialized because his rich appearing claim was actually pitifully poor and Volcanic City never grew beyond one building. Brown, however, was not deterred by this setback and in later years went on to considerable fortune when he staked some of the first ground on Copper Mountain. This fascinating prospector eventually ended his career when he disappeared on a trip up into the forbidding Pitt Lake country searching for the famous "Lost Slumach Mine."

The face of Brown's claim on Volcanic Mountain.

GOLD CREEKS

● Boundary Creek - This was the first gold creek to be found in the Boundary and was discovered in 1859 by American prospectors. It is a tributary of the Kettle River and flows into that river from the north-east. It was heavily mined in the first decade after its discovery and since then a number of individuals and companies have worked this stream by a variety of methods: rockers, ground sluicing, hydraulicking, etc. Chinese miners were also on the creek for years. The stretch of creek above Boundary Falls has long been considered barren; the best ground on the stream is from two to three miles above its junction with the Kettle river. The gold is often coarse and nuggets up to $50 have occasionally been recovered with most returns being found on a soft bedrock which averages around 18 feet in depth on the best section. Jack Thornton undoubtedly spent the longest time on the creek and did relatively well at times. Prospects: There are still places along this creek which bear study and even today snipers can make several dollars a day during low water. It is naturally spotty but there are several places where a sluicebox still yields average returns. A generally easy stream to work.

● July Creek - This stream lies west of Grand Forks and also flows into the Kettle river. It was discovered around 1860 and has yielded some fine

Tailings from an old shaft on Boundary Creek. Colours may still be panned along the banks of this historic placer gold stream.

gold for many years although nuggets over the $1 value are rare indeed. July Creek has been hydraulicked and there has been some drifting for old channels. Prospects: it was never considered an exceptional placer creek even in the early days, the gold is invariably fine and the chances of a worthwhile find are highly unlikely.

● Kettle River - This river is not usually considered a good placer river but there are several places worth noting. One spot three-quarters of a mile below the old Vernon-Edgewood Crossing on the east side has yielded some placer gold and nuggets ranging up to the $1.50 value. Another place which has given up gold is Cedar Creek, a small stream flowing into the Kettle from the west side about 12 miles north of Westbridge. Prospects: really not too promising although the river itself has yielded some gold from the bars in low water. The gold, however, is uniformly fine and not worth the effort required.

● Jolly Creek - This stream south of Conkle Lake merges with Rock Creek and has been worked since its discovery in 1860. Drifting, hydraulicking and other methods of mining have all yielded returns with some companies and individuals doing extremely well. The best gold is found on bedrock although there is some water trouble in places. The gold runs coarse and good sized nuggets have been found. Prospects: Jolly Creek, especially at and near its mouth will probably continue to yield placer gold for some years to come. It is considered to be a good gold creek even today and a careful prospector could still find worthwhile ground along this stream.

● May Creek - This stream is a tributary of July Creek and joins that creek about five miles west of Grand Forks. Like July Creek, the placer gold from this creek is generally fine and nuggets the exception rather than the rule. Returns have been less than encouraging from most of the operations undertaken on this creek. Prospects: fairly poor. It would be remarkable if there was any really worthwhile ground on this creek. Only the benches offer relatively poor possibilities.

● McKinney Creek - This is one of the main tributaries of Rock Creek and flows into that stream from the west joining it approximately ½ mile above the present highway bridge. The best ground was from the junction up to Rice Creek. Coarse gold was recovered in the first years by both Chinese and whites who worked this creek. There is considerable evidence of old workings all along this stream for some miles. Prospects: fairly good for a creek which has been worked as much as this one. Still possibilities of old channels although the first prospectors also considered this theory and did considerable prospecting with this in mind.

● Rice Creek - A small creek which flows into Mckinney Creek from the east. Some work has been done from time to time especially near the mouth of this stream. Some interesting returns on occasion although not usually as good as McKinney. Prospects: certainly not as good as several of the other tributaries of Rock Creek but still worth looking at.

● Pass Creek - This stream flows into the Granby river some 11 miles north of Grand Forks. Prospects: not very encouraging. The placer gold is fine and the likelihood of discovering good ground must be considered unlikely.

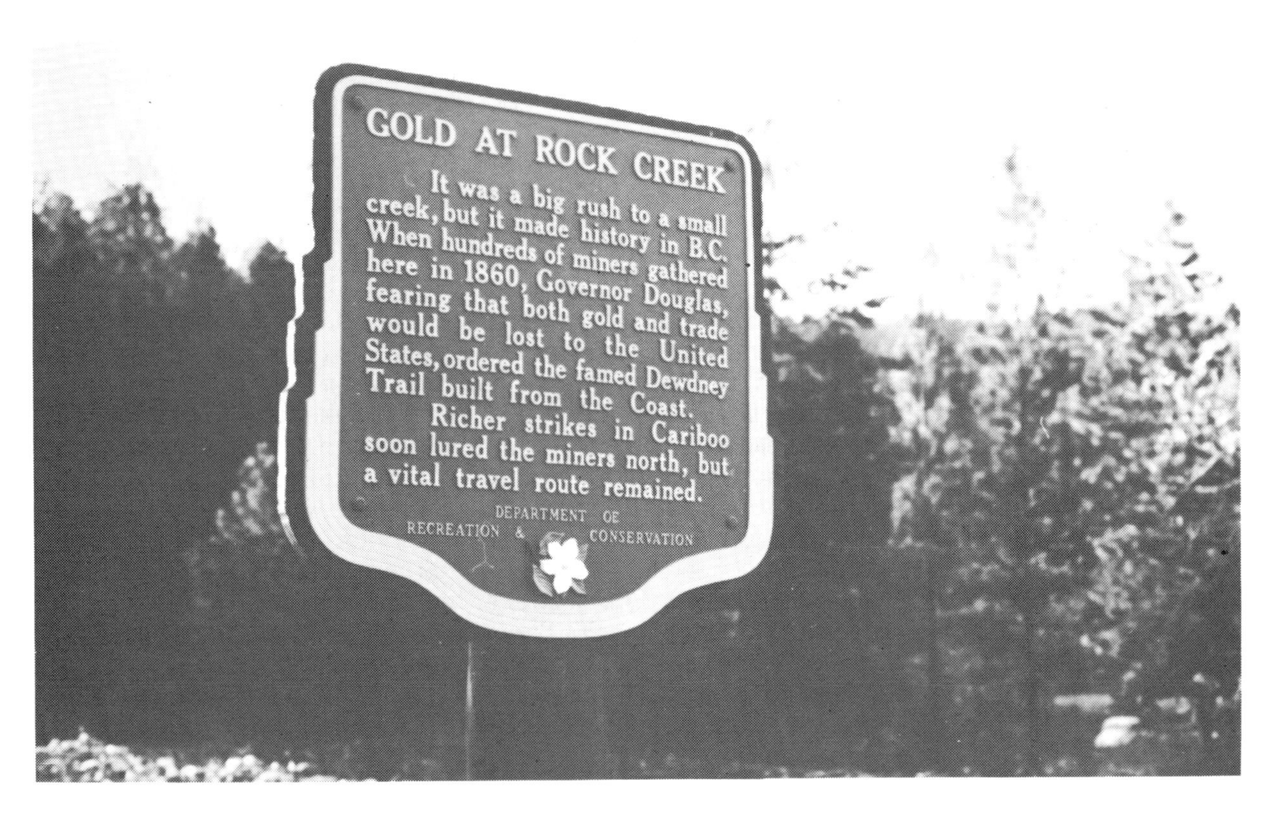

Historic marker at the village of Rock Creek.

Looking north and upstream toward the junction of McKinney and Rock creeks. For almost five miles upstream it is placer gold ground.

● Rock Creek - This stream is undoubtedly the most renowned placer gold creek in the Boundary Country. Discovered in 1859 by a Canadian named Adam Beam it was first known as York Creek. In his first six weeks on this creek Beam earned $977 with a rocker when the gold was bringing only $16 an ounce. It has been estimated that well over $250,000 in placer gold was recovered from the gravels along this creek although the true amount will never be known because much of the gold went over the U.S. line and never did reach the hands of the official purchasers. It was an extremely rich creek for many miles of its length and some of the bars like Soldier's, Denver, White's and others proved to be bonanzas. The two best sections on the entire creek were from its mouth upstream several miles and from the junction with Baker Creek up the creek for another five miles. An unusual creek in many respects; there were two distinct paystreaks with two types of gold; one was a lemon yellow and the other a coppery gold. The gold was recovered from both the hardpan and from bedrock with coarse gold quite common. The largest nugget recovered from Rock Creek was valued at nearly $150 although a number of pieces weighing over an ounce have been found all through its history. This stream was worked extensively from 1860 to about 1864 when there were at least 500 miners on its banks. It was again worked in the 1890's and again in the 1930's. Both whites and Chinese were active all along the creek for years with Jimmy Copeland probably being on the creek longer than anyone else. Prospects: Good. A stream with the reputation of Rock cannot be passed up. Some of the benches have proven to be good ground in the past and although this creek has been wing-dammed, hydraulicked, ground sluiced, drifted and generally well worked, it is still a good bet for the prospector who is prepared to study its history and its peculiar characteristics.

An hydraulic operation along Rock Creek in the late 1890's. Notice the water from the jet in the center.

INDIAN COUNTRY

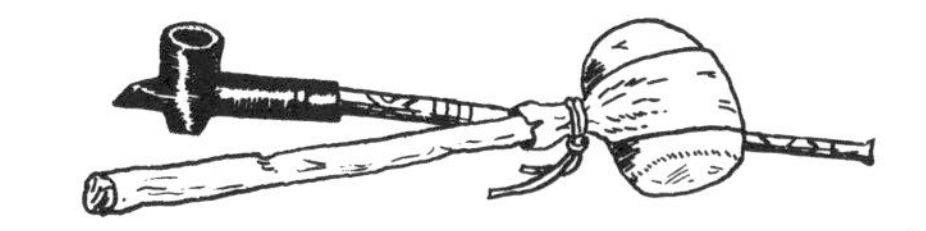

The Boundary region was not inhabited to the extent of either the Okanagan to the west or the Kootenays to the east and it is not generally recognized as Indian country today.

There were, nevertheless, several areas in the Boundary which were favoured by the Indians and other sections which were heavily traveled.

The most consistently occupied region was probably Christina Lake which had two major villages and at least a score of minor camps along its shores. One large village was located at the head of the lake on the east side of Sandner Creek; another major habitation place was at the foot of the lake, west of the Christina Creek outlet. Many artifacts have been recovered from both of these sites for years, as well as at lesser campsite locations at places like LaValley, Texas, English and other points and natural camping spots on the lake. There are also three pictograph location sites on rock faces on both sides of this remembered lake.

The canyon at Cascade was a prime salmon fishing location once, and remained so until Grand Coulee Dam was built. The Nez Perce from Colville trekked into this spot until after the turn of the century to spear the salmon near the canyon mouth. Evidence of their passing was unearthed several years ago when burials were discovered below the canyon on the west side of the Kettle river and other graves were found on the flats on the Cascade townsite.

The area between Cascade and Grand Forks was lightly settled although

The Kettle river canyon near Cascade. It was once a noted Indian fishing place before the salmon runs ceased after Grand Coulee Dam was erected.

there are indications that the original Indian horse trail was well used by the Salish up until the beginning of the 19th century. Several burial places were also found in this area; one on the original golf course at Grand Forks and another just west of the old Overhead Bridge about six miles east of the town.

There were also a number of places along the Kettle river between Midway and Rock Creek - this was open range country, the river was usually easy to ford and it was ideal for travel by horse. Rings of stone from tipis were still discernible in Midway in 1898 and much of the flats there were used as a campsite and grazing grounds. Near the mouths of several creeks on the south side of the river from three to four miles west of Midway there were kekuli depressions which were visible until 1969.

Rock Creek was also an old camping spot for hunters and there was a considerable base camp there at one time and a set of pictographs on the opposite side of the river attests to the presence of the Indians.

There are also other places in the Boundary which the Salish Indians frequented at one time or another but for some unknown reason, the entire region was uninhabited when the first whites arrived early in the 19th century.

Although little archaeological work has been carried on in the area, half a dozen burial sites and other evidence indicates that it was visited regularly at one time. Evidently the Indian population was decimated, possibly by plague from the lower Columbia river, and the region was then virtually abandoned. Today there are no Indians natural to the Boundary in the entire area and only their vacated campsites offer mute evidence that they once passed this way.

A few Boundary Indian artifacts from the Canada West Collection. These items were recovered from a number of different sites in the area.

TREASURE TROVE

JOLLY JACK'S LOST LODE

This account has been taken from N.L. Barlee's "Prospector's and Collector's Guide" which is now out of print. It is a relatively well known treasure story concerning a lost placer claim in the Boundary area.

His last name was Thornton although he was usually known as "Jolly Jack." He was a genuine prospector, one of the old breed, and he knew the Boundary Country like his own back yard for he had prospected all the old placer gold creeks; from Boundary Creek west to famous Rock Creek.

For years he had only limited success until somewhere in his travels he came across a rich placer - a placer which yielded coarse gold.

The location and even the existence of this gold placer have been the subject of much speculation. Most clues indicate that it was somewhere in the immediate vicinity of his cabin on Boundary Creek and was probably on that creek, but many old timers insist that it was on another stream nearby like Jolly Jack, Norwegian or even Rock Creek.

Thornton did, for many years, make his headquarters on Boundary Creek

Jolly Jack Thornton's cabin still stands on Boundary Creek and somewhere in the vicinity, according to the old story, is his lost placer mine.

but he also prospected on other streams close by and on occasion would turn up with a very heavy poke of coarse gold and when questioned about its source, the usually loquacious Thornton would become reticent.

Thornton never did reveal the location of his mysterious placer and his coarse gold nuggets and until his death continued to come up with the rich pokes from time to time. Thornton's old cabin still stands on a flat across Boundary Creek but the mystery of his lost placer mine has never been solved. Somewhere, tucked into a narrow draw or down a rocky gulch it's probably still there, waiting, as it has for decades for another fortunate prospector to stumble across it once again.

In examining the details of this treasure story it is sometimes almost impossible to unravel the facts from the ever present embellishments. There are, however, certain points which should be considered.

Various people who knew Thornton well contend that he did not have any secret placer. Others are equally vehement that he did have an unknown claim and state as proof that the coarse gold in his poke after certain absences was definitely not Boundary Creek gold. Gold does vary from creek to creek and an expert can often tell which creek it comes from simply by looking at it.

It is quite possible that Jack Thornton could have stumbled across a previously undiscovered spot on one of his many trips. If he did, however, it does seem likely that it was in the neighbourhood of Boundary Creek as he spent the bulk of his mining years on that creek.

The entire region has a number of gold creeks: May, July, Boundary, Rock, McKinney, Jolly, Rice and others, any one of which could be the stream. It is not entirely unreasonable to assume that Thornton did have a lost placer from which he drew nuggets from time to time and if he did it most probably still lies there undisturbed in its original location.

THE LOST GOLD BARS OF CAMP McKINNEY

This account was taken from the Summer, 1970, issue of "Canada West Magazine." Only some of the photographs are different.

This is a story about a bandit, his death and two cached gold bars which have lain undetected for three-quarters of a century in a remote corner of the Boundary Country.

Although some of the details concerning the celebrated hold-up in 1896 and the subsequent death of the highwayman still remain shrouded after many decades, the basic information is accurate and may eventually lead to the recovery of the lost bullion.

In 1896, a little gold mining town known as Camp McKinney, situated on the south-eastern slopes of towering Baldy Mountain, had come into existence on the strength of several mines in the area. The premier mine of the group was the Cariboo-Amelia, usually referred to simply as the Cariboo. It was a mining operation so successful that in slightly more than two years it had paid out in excess of $100,000 to its shareholders.

It was the custom at this mine to pour several gold bricks each month and then take the bullion east by wagon to the small town of Midway where it was then trans-shipped to the United States.

On August 18, 1896, George B. McAulay of Spokane, one of the major shareholders in the Cariboo Mine, stepped into a wagon in Camp McKinney - his destination was Midway and in a saddle-bag in the back of the wagon were three gold bricks with a total weight of over 600 ounces. Although the price of gold ran only $20 an ounce at the time, the shipment was valued at more than $10,000. As usual, there was no shotgun guard with McAulay as it was widely assumed that a hold-up would never be risked in that high country.

it was a logical assumption because McKinney was located in rough terrain, an area crosscut by canyons and cliffs and the few roads and trails leading into the gold camp were easily closed off in case of robbery.

So McAulay, disregarding ordinary precautions, set off down the road toward Midway. A quarter of an hour later, just as the shareholder was rounding a bend on the narrow road, a masked man stepped out in front of the wagon brandishing a rifle. Reigning to an abrupt stop, the driver was gruffly ordered to throw out the saddlebag. Looking down the barrel of a levelled Winchester, McAulay complied with the order and threw the gold-laden saddlebag onto the dusty road. With a menacing wave of his rifle, the hold-up man then told the driver to keep on going.

McAulay didn't require much urging and as soon as he was out of sight he quickly whipped his team to a fast pace and made Midway in good time. Once there, he immediately informed Constables Dinsmore and McMynn of the

The hold-up of the gold wagon took place on the old stage road near here in 1896. This is the original road with McMynn's Meadows beyond. It has been the theory of many that the gold bars still lie in this vicinity.

hold-up. The two Provincial Policemen left at once for Camp McKinney and within a few hours all avenues of escape had been closed off and guards posted to watch all trails and roads leading out of the gold camp. Every outgoing rider and stage was checked to make sure that the missing gold wasn't being smuggled out of the area.

A careful search of the robbery area revealed only the empty saddle-bag and two drained whiskey bottles. There were no good clues.

Within a few days the Cariboo Mining Company had posted a total of $3,500 in reward money for information leading to the recovery of the gold and the capture of the unknown bandit.

Shortly after, James Monaghan, one of the mine owners, received an anonymous letter from an individual who claimed to have travelled to Camp McKinney with a drifter who went by the name, Matt Roderick. The unidentified letter writer went on to say that he had first met Roderick in a saloon in Oroville, a border town in the state of Washington, in May of 1896 and that Roderick had suggested at that time that they "knock off" the McKinney gold wagon. The correspondent stated that he had gone to Camp McKinney with Roderick but had drifted on to Trail Creek (Rossland) shortly after and had learned of the hold-up in the "Spokesman Review."

Acting on this lead, it was soon ascertained that a man by the name of Roderick had indeed worked at McKinney and furthermore, on the day of the robbery, he had been absent from work claiming that he was ill and had supposedly stayed in his cabin. It was also discovered that Roderick several days after the hold-up had quit his job, stating ill-health as his reason. He had left camp by stagecoach but, according to witnesses, he had pulled out with little luggage and nothing as heavy as gold bars.

Eventually Roderick was traced to Seattle where he was kept under surveillance. He wasn't arrested because of lack of proof and also because the mine owners were sure that he would eventually return to the camp to retrieve the hidden gold bars. It was arranged to have Roderick shadowed all the time he remained in Seattle.

Finally, in the latter half of October, he left Seattle by train for the interior of Washington and eventually disembarked near Concully where he purchased a fine dapple grey horse. Continually moving north, he left Loomis and headed over the Canadian border for Camp McKinney. It was the 24th of October.

Unknown to Roderick, he was being watched, and when he finally turned east and moved into the Okanagan country it was reported to the officers of the Cariboo Mine.

An Indian constable called Long Alex and Tom Graham were immediately dispatched to watch at the forks of Anarchist Mountain and the Fairview Road and ordered to report back if and when Roderick appeared.

On the evening of October 26, 1896, their quarry was reported to be heading toward Camp McKinney and R.W. Deans and Joseph Keane, the manager of the Cariboo Mine, set out along the road to intercept the suspect.

It had previously been decided that they were to stop Roderick, even if it meant shooting his horse from under him, then capture him and return him to McKinney for interrogation.

Events, however, were to prove far different in the hectic few minutes which followed. As the two made their way along the road darkness began to close and the half-light made visibility difficult. A few minutes passed and then an indistinct figure on horseback loomed up ahead of them.

Deans, under oath, later testified:

> ...after walking about a mile I became aware that there was some object on the road; we both supposed that it was the Indian (Long

Alex) returning; it was too dark to distinguish what the object was; after walking a short distance further I could see the object on the road was a grey horse. I stepped to one side of the road supposing Mr. Keane had done the same until a few moments later I heard him speak to Roderick saying, 'Is that you, Matt?' Roderick made no answer for perhaps half a minute; a moment later the shot was fired...Roderick seemed to jump across the road; thinking he had shot Mr. Keane I fired at him with my rifle but missed him. Mr. Keane then spoke and said 'I have shot him; I had to do it or he would have shot me; he had his rifle levelled at my breast...'

Roderick's body lay sprawled in the middle of the road - the bandit had died instantly from Keane's single shot. His clothes were searched and only a purse with $9.10 in it and two small chips of gold which were found carefully wrapped in a piece of writing paper were recovered.

Although an inquest was held later and Keane subsequently tried for manslaughter, no further light was shed on the whereabouts of the lost gold bars - evidently the secret of the lost bullion died with Roderick.

Almost three-quarters of a century has elapsed since the robbery and the death of the mysterious Roderick, and the bricks, now valued at more than $20,000, are undoubtedly still cached in the area - somewhere close by the old road, probably between McMynn's Meadows and the remains of old Camp McKinney. And someday, some tenderfoot will probably stumble across them, still in their original hiding place in the high country near the gold camp once called McKinney.

Note* - There are several theories concerning this treasure story which should be considered as they tend to clarify certain apparent weaknesses in the account. These theories are dealt with on the following page.

McDuff's Shoeing Shop in Midway in the late 1890's. Constables Dinsmore and McMynn set out from here when they heard news of the robbery.

● There is considerable evidence that Roderick did manage to smuggle out the smallest of the gold bricks with him when he left Camp McKinney shortly after the robbery. It is generally assumed that the bandit cached the two largest bricks somewhere near the hold-up scene to be retrieved at a later and more convenient date. The two pieces of gold found in his pocket at the time of his death were probably from the small brick.

● Many old-timers insist that Roderick was wearing a smuggler's vest when he was shot and killed. This vest was purportedly divided into two pockets, each pocket designed to hold a large gold brick. Unfortunately, this theory has never been proven and must still be considered conjecture as neither the court records nor the report of Constables McMynn and Dinsmore mention the existence of a vest.

● There is a widely held assumption and probably a logical one; that Roderick buried the gold somewhere between the hold-up site and the gold camp. Roderick, despite his obvious faults, was relatively well educated and evidently intelligent, it does not seem reasonable to assume that he would take the unnecessary risk of carrying the bullion with him for any length of time after the hold-up took place. Therefore, the most logical place to hide the gold would be within a few minutes riding distance of McMynn's Meadows.

● There have also been hints of collusion between Roderick and certain shareholders of the Cariboo Mine. Again, this has been researched and it seems that neither Keane nor McAulay displayed any unusual indications of sudden wealth after the death of Roderick. In Keane's case, seemingly the most logical suspect, the exact opposite seems true.

● After weighing all the available evidence, it seems highly possible that the stolen bullion still rests in its old spot although the chance of it being recovered in that terrain would have to be considered rather unlikely. Even the most dedicated treasure hunter would be compelled to admit that the Lost Gold Bars of Camp McKinney will likely remain lost.

This is the west road between Camp McKinney and Fairview. It was on this road that Matthew Roderick met his death on his return to the camp to retrieve the buried gold bars.

The town of Ainsworth on Kootenay Lake. This photograph shows the camp as it looked before the devastating fire of 1896.

THE WEST KOOTENAY

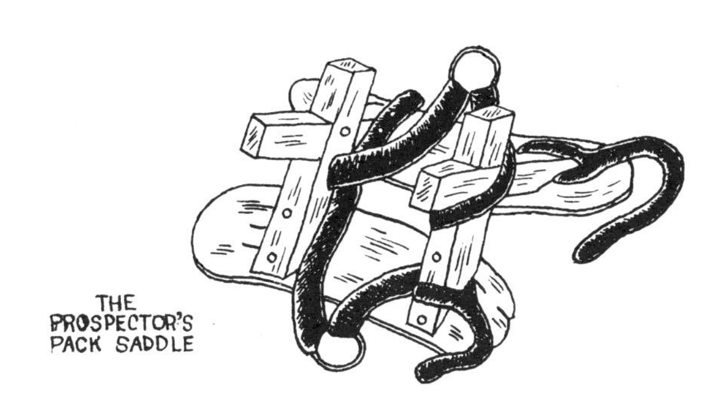

THE PROSPECTOR'S PACK SADDLE

INTRODUCTION

West Kootenay - This was where mining was king in the 1890's when those mining towns of yesteryear like Sandon, Rossland, Ainsworth, Cody, Slocan City, Silverton, Nelson and a host of others leapt to the forefront when illustrious mines like the LeRoi, Silver King, Blue Bell, Payne, War Eagle, Slocan Star and a hundred other banner producers sparked imaginations throughout the west.

From the towering Slocan country, south to the sandy benchlands of old Fort Shepherd, through the Indian country along the Slocan and Kootenay rivers and back beyond to forgotten towns like Ferguson, Camborne and Retallack. A land of haunting beauty, from wind-swept Kootenay Lake to the memorable Upper Arrow, an area where shadows still loom from another century in this ghost town country - the West Kootenay.

The old Windsor Hotel in Trout Lake City today.

GHOST TOWNS

AINSWORTH

In its earliest years it was known as Hot Springs Camp, for it was to this remote spot on the west side of vast Kootenay Lake that the Indians used to travel to bathe in the hot springs which they believed had great curative powers.

In 1882, George Ainsworth located the townsite which was renamed in honour of his father, Captain J.C. Ainsworth; a wealthy American mining and railway man who had shown great interest in the Kootenay country in the 1880's and 1890's.

Progress was slow in Ainsworth initially, for other townsites were competing and six years later only G.B. Wright's store had located on the townsite. Then the Slocan excitement drew attention away from it just when Ainsworth seemed on the verge of becoming more than just a one store town. Finally, when the wild rush to the Slocan subsided, some of the miners and promoters returned to re-examine the lead-silver properties nearby and by 1896 quite a little town had grown up by the lakeshore and a number

The mining men of Ainsworth in 1898. The notice on the bulletin board on the building on the near left states: "NOTICE - $1000 REWARD" and is more than likely a wanted poster.

1,000,000 pounds of rich silver-lead ore waiting to be shipped from the wharf at Ainsworth. The ore was hauled from the mines by ore wagons and then carried by stern-wheelers to the smelters. Circa 1898.

Ainsworth in 1898 after the disasterous fire of 1896. This remarkable photograph shows the main street of Ainsworth in that day; looking east towards Kootenay Lake with the Vancouver House and The Club in the foreground. The town was then considered to be on the climb.

of enterprising businessmen like Geigerich, McNeal and the Greens were competing for the continually increasing trade.

But disaster struck on the night of April 26, 1896, when a mysterious fire broke out in the McNeal building and quickly jumped to the huge hotel owned by the Ainsworth S.S. Co. and despit herculean efforts by fire-fighters, soon most of the business section was ablaze. When morning came two-thirds of the camp and every hotel had been razed. It was a stunning setback for the little town but one from which it rapidly recovered; and within months the town had been re-built.

By 1897, properties like the Pearl Lulu, Skyline, Highland, Jeff Davis and Mile Point studded the surrounding hills and their continual harvest of silver reflected on the prosperity of the town and soon Ainsworth was recognized as one of the main mining towns in the Kootenay.

Those vivid years continued until after the turn of the century, but mines are affected by the lottery of fate and their life span is always difficult to determine and too soon their reserves of paying ore ran out and, one by one, they terminated operations. And Ainsworth waned also and soon became not much more than a name as other towns like Kaslo and Nelson took its place.

Today, the McKinnon House, the Vancouver House, the Club and other retreats of the mining years have vanished but a few reminders of that era; like the Silver Ledge Hotel and an occasional false-front building still bring to mind the time when Ainsworth was "the town" on Kootenay Lake.

The Silver Ledge Hotel in Ainsworth in 1970.

CAMBORNE

Beyond the head of the Upper Arrow Lake and east of the Northeast Arm, past old Beaton and up a sometimes treacherous river called the Incomappleux are the remains of Camborne.

In the late 1890's, on the heels of the mining rush to the Kootenay country; many prospectors, unable to locate good claims in the heavily staked Slocan, fanned out to the north hoping to find other bonanzas. By 1900, a group of claims assaying high in gold had been staked near the mouth of Pool Creek and in short order a rough mining camp known as Fish Creek Camp came into being. The name Camborne soon replaced Fish Creek and within months, several hotels, three stores and a handful of houses made up what could be called a town.

Camborne looked promising, so much so, in fact, that the editor of the CAMBORNE MINER sounded the drum of optimism when properties like the Eva, Silver Dollar, Meridian, Gold Finch, Independence and dozens of others yielded high grade ore. Hopes surged again when several stamp mills were put into operation to handle the ore. For a decade the town boomed; with regular stages to Beaton and hotels like the Coronation keeping their doors open day and night to accomodate the influx.

So Camborne prospered until the zenith was reached and then passed as the ore output slowly dwindled. Soon the unmistakable signs indicated

An open stage leaving Camborne around the turn of the century.

This old photograph shows the rough terrain near Camborne. This is the road into the mining camp from Thompson's Landing in 1902.

Packing into the Silver Dollar Mine near Camborne in 1906.

that Camborne was beginning to slip; the stages came less frequently and eventually not at all and the hotels greeted fewer and fewer customers as the mining men began to avoid the area in preference for more promising regions. It became all too apparent that the town was dying.

Over the years there were revivals as base metals in the vicinity kept hopes flickering but when the last mine closed in 1958 even those optimists realized that Camborne had finally reached the end of the road.

Today, remnants of later camps still stand but of old Camborne little remains for it has become little more than a name.

CODY

It was founded to challenge mighty Sandon and Cody was its name. The plans were grandiose; a model town east of Sandon - with a railroad, a brewery, hotels, assay office, other business establishments and even a concentrator. The ore was close at hand and with mines like the illustrious Noble Five, American Boy and Last Chance, the prospects of success were never questioned.

Strangely, Cody never really got off the ground although it claimed 150 inhabitants at its height. Its tenure was brief and unobtrusive as Sandon soon eclipsed its brash rival and Cody crumbled and then vanished. It had been born with little fanfare and died with less, today it is difficult to imagine that a town ever stood on the site.

An early artist's view of Cody, B.C.

An original photograph of Cody in its early years showing the business section of the town and the Noble Five concentrator on the left.

Abandoned Cody today with more recent buildings on the old site.

ERIE

Several miles west of Salmo is the site of Erie. Originally known as North Fork, it was founded in the 1860's when placer miners discovered gold in a canyon on a stream called North Fork Creek, now known as Erie Creek. The town never amounted to much although it existed precariously for many years but finally declined when first Ymir and then Salmo came into their own.

The town of Erie in 1910. The declining years at the end of the placer rush to Erie Creek.

FERGUSON

Stand on the deserted flats late some night when the mountain winds drift down over the townsite; and you will then agree that there's something haunting about Ferguson.

It was a mining town deep in the Lardeau country at the turn of the century and in that day it was quite a place. Started with high expectations when ore deposits were discovered in the vicinity, the town began hitting its stride in 1897 when the plush Lardeau Hotel opened its doors; others soon followed and by 1899, its main street was lined with hotels,

Andy Daney's freight wagon crossing the bridge on Halfway Creek between Ferguson and Trout Lake City - 1902.

The Lardeau Hotel in Ferguson today.

saloons, general merchants and other businesses and fully 800 people made it their town.

Like most mining towns of consequence, it even had a newspaper; the FERGUSON EAGLE, and an eccentric editor with the rather unlikely name of Pettipiece, to boot. But newspapers were often indicators of fortune and when the EAGLE folded, Ferguson was already on the decline, and by 1920, all but a hardy few had left and it was no longer really a town.

Since then the years have been harsh and now only half a dozen old buildings remain on the townsite - and the Ferguson that once was lives on only in memory.

Main Street in Ferguson, B.C. - circa 1898.

A sketch of the original door of the jailhouse in Ferguson which is still standing on its original site.

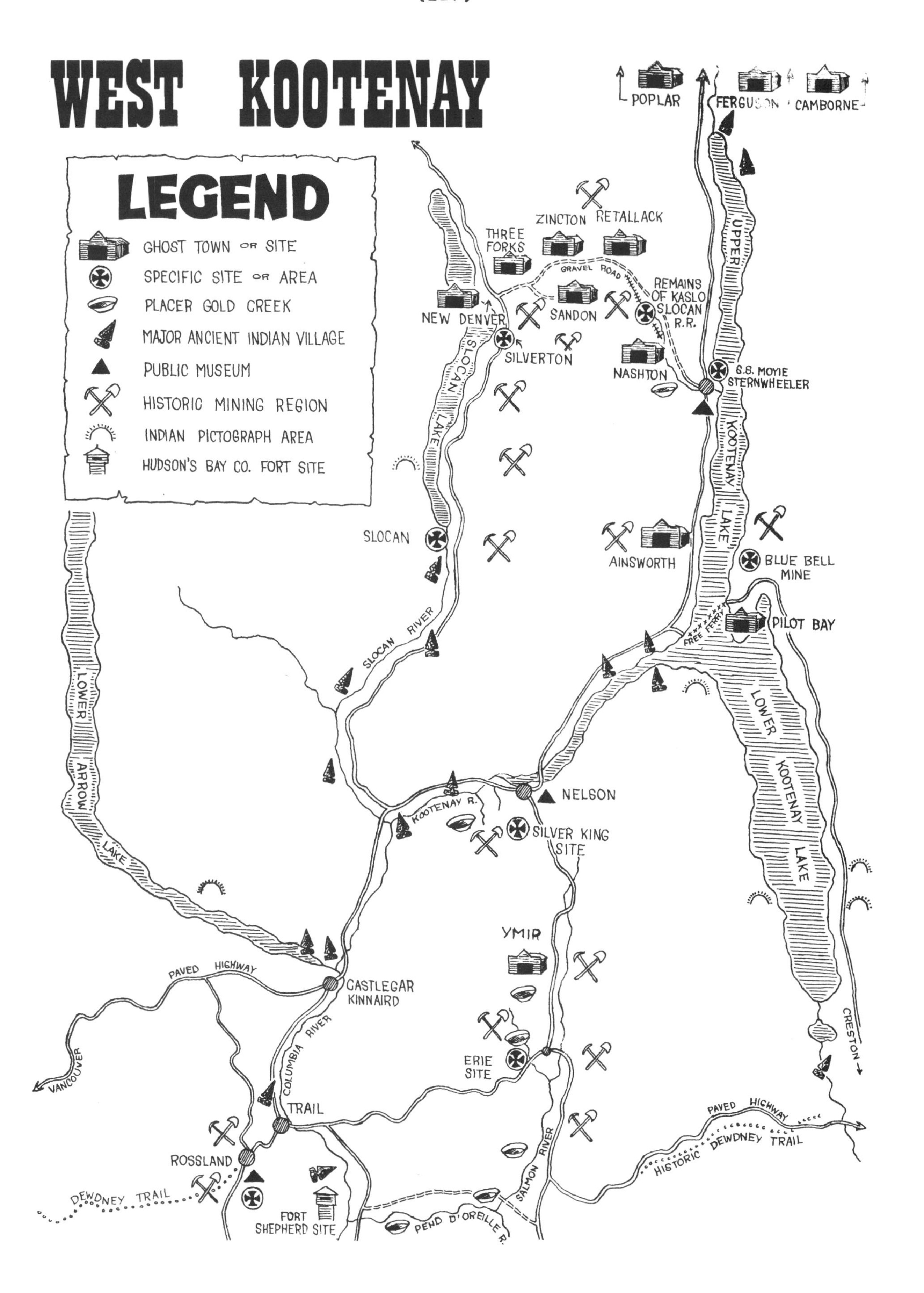
WEST KOOTENAY
LEGEND
GHOST TOWN OR SITE
SPECIFIC SITE OR AREA
PLACER GOLD CREEK
MAJOR ANCIENT INDIAN VILLAGE
PUBLIC MUSEUM
HISTORIC MINING REGION
INDIAN PICTOGRAPH AREA
HUDSON'S BAY CO. FORT SITE
POPLAR
FERGUSON
CAMBORNE
ZINCTON
RETALLACK
THREE FORKS
GRAVEL ROAD
REMAINS OF KASLO SLOCAN R.R.
NEW DENVER
SANDON
SILVERTON
NASHTON
S.S. MOYIE STERNWHEELER
UPPER
KOOTENAY
LAKE
SLOCAN
LAKE
SLOCAN
AINSWORTH
BLUE BELL MINE
PILOT BAY
FREE FERRY
SLOCAN RIVER
LOWER
KOOTENAY
LAKE
LOWER ARROW LAKE
NELSON
KOOTENAY R.
SILVER KING SITE
YMIR
CASTLEGAR KINNAIRD
PAVED HIGHWAY
COLUMBIA RIVER
CRESTON
VANCOUVER
ERIE SITE
TRAIL
PAVED HIGHWAY
HISTORIC DEWDNEY TRAIL
ROSSLAND
SALMON RIVER
DEWDNEY TRAIL
FORT SHEPHERD SITE
PEND D'OREILLE R.

KASLO

In its day Kaslo was the eastern gateway to the "Silvery Slocan," and in the hectic mining years of the 1890's it was to this wide open town that the sternwheelers came with their decks jammed with eager prospectors and piled high with supplies. It was from Kaslo that the quaint Kaslo-Slocan Railway built its winding narrow gauge line into the precipitous Slocan country to challenge the formidable Canadian Pacific Railway for ore shipment rights.

Surprisingly, Kaslo wasn't a mining town like nearby Whitewater or Sandon, it was the center of commerce of the mining area and its business was primarily freighting and supplying. It tended its business well and by 1893 it became an incorporated city and claimed a population of nearly 1,500. Like other towns in the region, much of its prosperity hinged on silver and in years like 1893 when the price of that metal dropped to 75¢ an ounce, the town was hard hit and nobody was harder hit than the editor of the KASLO CLAIM, the inimitable Robert Tecumseh Lowery. Lowery, along with many others was bankrupted in the business decline and in the August 25, 1893 issue of the Claim, the front page was bordered in black and in the center of the page was a tombstone - on it was the epitaph:

BUSTED BY GOSH
"Keep off the grass. Sacred to the memory of the Kaslo Claim.
Born May 12, 1893, died August 25, 1893. Aged sixteen weeks.
Let her R.I.P."

Calathumpian Parade along busy Front Street in Kaslo City in 1894.

An open stagecoach in front of Garland's Store in Kaslo in 1893. This was the stage used on the regular run to Sandon and the silver country.

Two sternwheelers tie up near Kaslo in 1901. They were the city's only link with the outside until the west-side road was finally built.

The Langham Hotel as it stands in Kaslo today.

This is the flood of 1894 when the waters of Kootenay Lake rose to more than 28 feet above low water level and destroyed more than six dozen of the town's dwellings and businesses.

From the editor who published unpaid advertisements upside down and partially paid ones sideways - it was a fitting farewell to a colourful town. But Kaslo survived, even when it was subjected to both a towering fire and a devastating flood in 1894 and remained active long after the mining era had subsided and other towns close by had disappeared.

Its main street was once as impressive as its inhabitants when nearly twenty hotels like the Hotel Slocan, Palace, Grand Northern, Leland, Silver King and others lined Front Street and over half a hundred other businesses catered to the many needs of its diverse population.

Today, the boom has long ended but Kaslo is still there and so are a few of the reminders of the silver years; the sternwheeler "Moyie" after sixty years of service to the city lies at anchor on the lakeshore and a few of the once many buildings, like the old Langham Hotel, still stand as a tribute to those years.

NEW DENVER

First known as Eldorado, it became New Denver after Denver, Colorado, when it was anticipated that it would eventually become a greater mining town than its namesake. Although never as large as Kaslo or even Slocan City, it was advantageously placed - on the eastern side of Slocan Lake on a flat and pleasant delta at the mouth of Carpenter Creek which was the natural route into the silver country.

By 1893, it claimed 250 permanent residents and a shifting population

Near the waterfront in New Denver. The original Newmarket Hotel is visible on the right. This hotel, which opened its doors for business in 1893 is still operating and is one of a number of frontier buildings in the town.

New Denver in the early 1890's.

The bar room of the St. Jame's Hotel in New Denver - circa 1898.

which sometimes ran to twice that number. Close by, silver-lead properties like the Mountain Chief, Alpha, California, Idaho - Cumberland and Alamo contributed to the general prosperity of the town. Before the decade was out, a number of hotels like the Newmarket, St. James, Denver, Central and Windsor greeted incoming mining men and a school, the Bank of Montreal, livery stables, general stores, a newspaper and dozens of other business enterprises lent the town an air of respectability.

With the boats landing daily at the waterfront, the C.P.R. building their line and then running into Sandon and Three Forks, and the silver excitement with its continuous fluctuations; it was a spirited town for almost two decades.

Today the mining activity has lessened and New Denver isn't the busy center it once was but it has retained much of its old atmosphere; the Newmarket is still there down by the waterfront, the Bank of Montreal's original building stands yet as do a dozen other time worn structures of those bygone days when New Denver was considered the new Eldorado.

NASHTON OR ZWICKY

At the confluence of Keen Creek and the clear Kaslo river there is a natural site for a town and in late 1896, a stopping place called South Fork was erected there. The line of the Kaslo-Slocan Railway passed through the town on its way to Sandon and when silver mines in the vicinity like

The place originally known as South Fork and later called either Zwicky or Nashton. Active as a shipping center for the mines nearby from 1897 to 1918, this is all that remains of the town today.

THE SLOCAN IN 1897

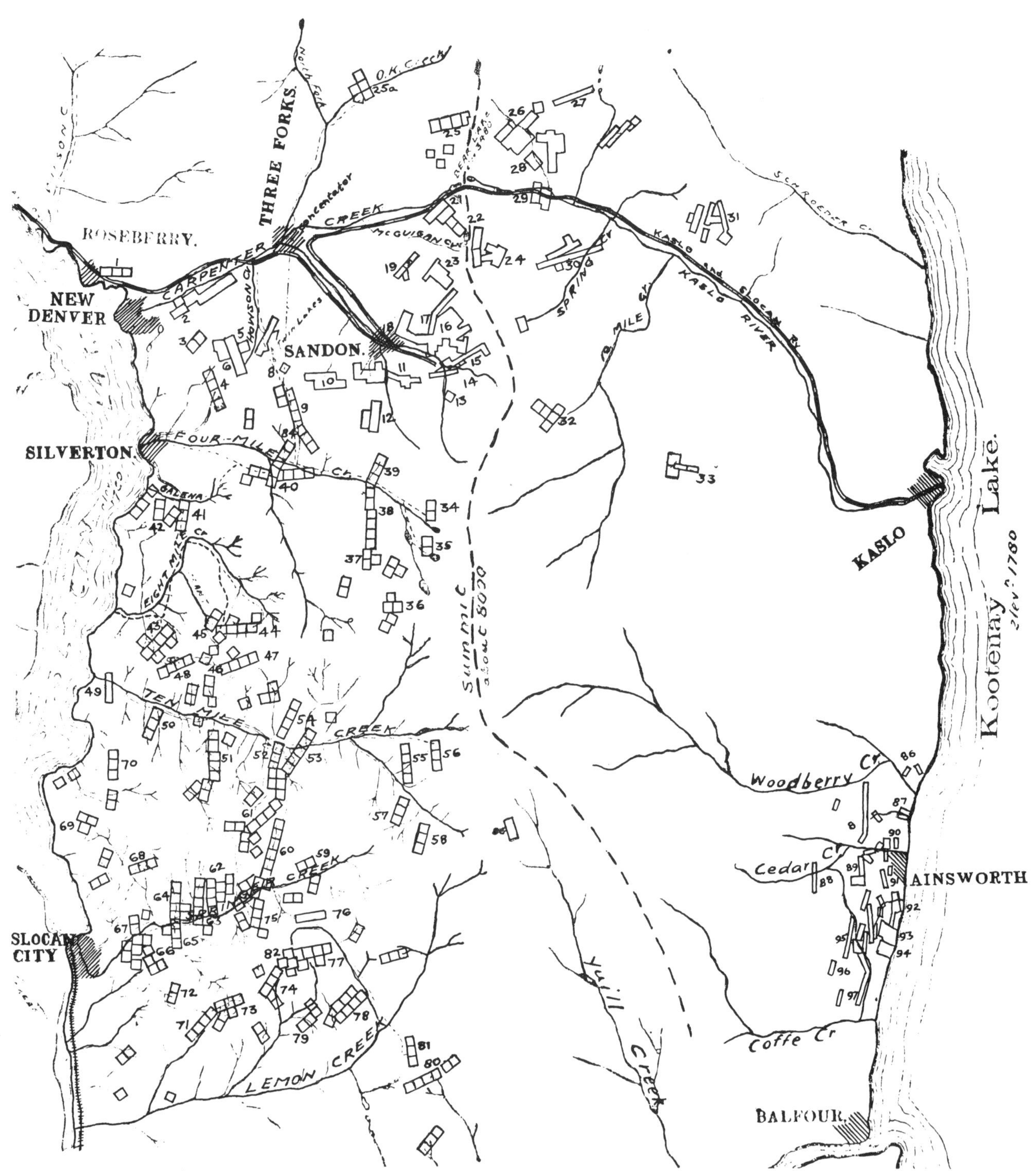

This is Webster Brown's map of the Slocan region in 1897, showing the mining towns and claims in the area which are all numbered. The majority of the silver properties are located on the western side of the summit except in the immediate areas of Ainsworth and Retallack.

the Alice-Utica, Cork-Province and Montezuma began producing, South Fork became the logical shipping center for these mines and its name was changed to Zwicky.

A hotel, several stores and a handful of houses completed the town in 1898 and it maintained its place as the flow of ore continued. In 1915, it was honoured with a post office and the name Nashton. It was a durable place and it lasted for several more decades, just as long as the mines did.

Now the stagecoaches of Scott, Baker and Company no longer make the run past to Retallack and beyond and the Kaslo-Slocan Railway line has been abandoned these many years and Nashton is deserted too - only the shell of this thrice named town remains, barely recognizeable today.

PILOT BAY

In a secluded bay on the eastern side of Kootenay Lake is a ghost smelter - Pilot Bay.

It's an unlikely place for a smelter, far off the beaten track, close to a headland overlooking the grandeur of the lake but it was once a massive operation.

In the early 1890's, the Hendryx interests conceived the idea of a smelter on the east side of Kootenay Lake to treat the ores from their Blue Bell lead-silver mine at Riondel. By 1895 the Pilot Bay Smelter was in operation. In that inuagural year, the company employed almost 200 men

The Pilot Bay Smelter at the height of its operations in 1895.

and the town which grew up around the complex had 1,000 inhabitants, four hotels, three stores and a few other businesses. As well as the celebrated Blue Bell, a number of Ainsworth mines and a few in the Slocan shipped their rich ore to the smelter for treatment.

But the end was close, for by 1896, the Hall Mines smelter in Nelson blew in their first furnaces and this formidable competitor immediately began siphoning off much of the revenue producing ore from the region. This, coupled with high transportation costs, resulted in the unexpected closure of the plant at Pilot Bay in that same year.

For a decade it lay idle until it was finally re-opened in 1905 and operated intermittently for some years thereafter. But it was never a paying proposition and when it closed the second time it was permanent.

The smelter stands in isolated ruins now, a sad salute to an ill-fated dream. And in the underbrush, almost unnoticed, are the remnants of the town; decaying lumber, a few bricks, an occasional bottle or a solitary coin dropped by an unknown hand three-quarters of a century ago, when the "big operation" was at Pilot Bay.

The ruins of the smelter at Pilot Bay today.

POPLAR

The postcard is faded now but you can still make out the townsite and the lettering beneath:

"View of the town of Poplar, B.C.
famous for its rich, free gold quartz, arsenical and telluride gold ores. Situated on the Canadian Pacific Railway, 23 miles north of the twon of Lardeau at the head of Kootenai Lake, B.C."

Gold was discovered on the right-of-way of the Arrowhead and Kootenay Railway early in 1903 and immediately Poplar or Poplar Creek came into existence. It really only lasted for a little more than a year but such were the expectations that within days four hotels and several stores had been erected along one side of the only street on the townsite.

Not unexpectedly, R.T. Lowery, of Kootenay newspaper fame established a short-lived paper called the POPLAR CREEK NUGGET and passed his usual wry comments on the town and its inhabitants. But when Lowery left, Poplar had run its course; the anticipated gold rush never materialized and the ore was not as good as the advertisements said it was and in short order Poplar became a spent town.

Now there are only a few log cabins and the remains of hotels like the Royal and Commercial to greet the eye. You could easily pass by Poplar - almost everyone else did nearly seventy years ago.

RETALLACK OR WHITEWATER

High up in the divide near the 3500 foot level stands old Retallack. Quite a name, quite a camp.

It was later on the scene than Sandon or Kaslo but when a prospector named Kamplan staked an iron stain showing and succeeded in selling it to J. Eaton for $200, the latter sunk a pick into the outcrop and it proved to be almost solid galena. Eaton contented himself with taking out almost a million dollars in ore and a new camp was born.

The remains of Whitewater or Retallack today, still standing high up in the pass between Kaslo and Sandon in that fascinating silver country.

The concentrator at Whitewater in 1899.

The mining town of Whitewater in 1898.

There is still an aura about Whitewater or Retallack. No-one lives there now but it's a picturesque area; with the abandoned remains of the Kaslo-Slocan Railway still clinging to the cliffside above the fast flowing Kaslo River, the slowly decaying buildings on the flats and the old mine workings close by. It's a remembered place.

SANDON

Some towns cast a lingering spell and down their streets history still walks - it does in Sandon.

When they speak of ghost towns the name of Sandon always comes to the fore. It had that special and perhaps intangible air that only a few towns possess. It had it all - great mines, iron men, triumphs, disasters and that unique quality sometimes called colour.

Even its beginning had style. In the fall of 1891, two prospectors, Eli Carpenter and John Seaton, returning to Ainsworth after an uneventful prospecting trip north of Slocan Lake took a shortcut through a previously unmapped mountainous region east of the lake. And fate was looking over their shoulders for as they struggled to the top of an unnamed 7100 foot mountain they accidently stumbled across an outcrop of ore - silver ore

The famous "Big Boulder," found by J.W. Cockle on July 14, 1892. The excited discoverer immediately staked the entire region around the rock. He then sold the 125 ton rock for $2,000 and it yielded $20,000 in silver to its purchaser. Cockle lost again when it was later found that the almost solid galena boulder had rolled down the mountainside from the Slocan Star property and his valued claim was worthless.

Bartlett's pack train on its way through Sandon - circa 1896.

Sandon as it looked in 1895. Visible in this photograph are both the Denver Hotel and the office of the newspaper, the Paystreak.

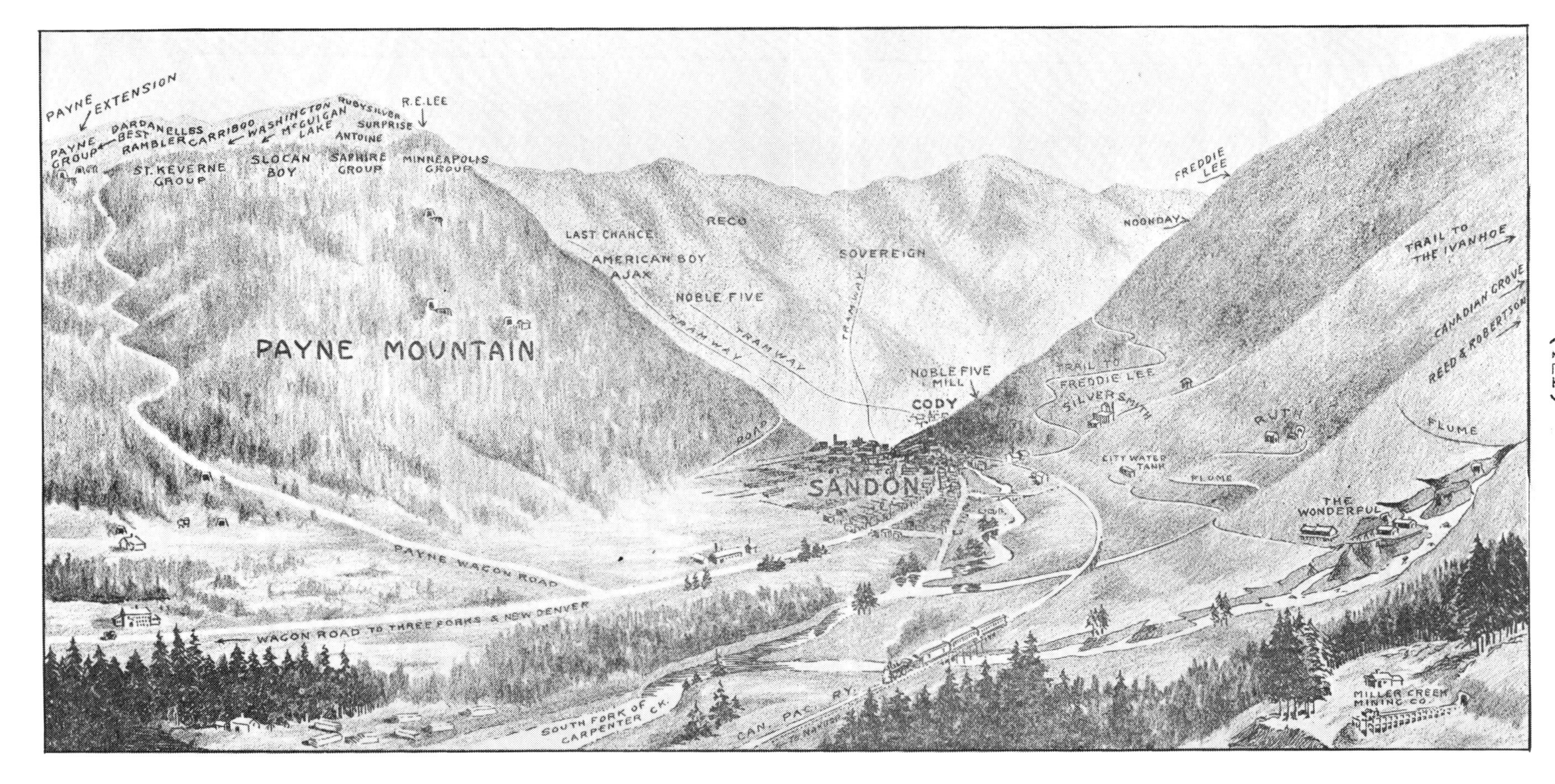

This sketch of the Sandon area was part of a stock promotion deal nearly half a century ago. Although the basic information is generally accurate, the artist's conception of the region near Sandon gives a misleading idea of spaciousness to the unsuspecting would-be stock purchaser.

Sandon in 1896 with rival railroads on either side of the gulch.

Sandon in 1898. The main street is on the left side of Carpenter Creek.

that looked so rich that they excitedly broke off some samples and hastily beat their way back to Ainsworth. Once there, Carpenter took the samples to be assayed while his unsuspecting partner waited anxiously. Several days passed before the greatly anticipated assay reports were given to Seaton and he was dumbfounded when he read them: the assays indicated that the rich looking ore was virtually worthless. Dismayed, Seaton made his way to a saloon nearby to contemplate his poor fortune, unaware that the crafty Carpenter had switched ore samples on him.

As the despondent prospector sat drinking to his ill-luck, he was approached by the proprietor who cautiously advised him that Carpenter had been overheard making plans with John Sandon and others for a return trip to the mountain. Outraged, the resolute Seaton acted quickly and had soon gathered together four Irishmen; Hennessey, Hennessey, McGuigan and Flint. The men swore a partnership and called themselves the Noble Five.

Although Carpenter had already left, the five prospectors set off up the west side of Kootenay Lake. At the Kaslo river they turned west once more . Struggling up through the tangled undergrowth in that draw they found the mountain and located their claims; and the claim which became the most celebrated of that rich group was named - the Noble Five.

Kaslo-Slocan locomotive and train crossing the 31 Bridge at Falls Cr. near Payne Bluff on the K & S line approaching Sandon. This photograph taken in 1910 gives one some idea of the rugged terrain through which the railways were compelled to build in order to reach Sandon and the silver country.

This strike signalled a frantic rush to the area and by 1892, one of the great silver regions on the continent flashed into prominence - The Silvery Slocan.

Soon, other illustrious finds were made and notable properties came into production: the Slocan Boy, later known as the Slocan Star, a mine whose ore body was so massive that it measured a full fifty feet between the walls; and the Reco-Goodenough, whose ore yielded a fantastic four hundred and seven ounces of silver and forty two per cent lead per ton, and the famous Payne Boy, after known simply as the Payne, which made over $4,000,000 in its first decade of operation. There were others like the Monitor, Rambler-Cariboo, Mammoth and scores more whose names still stand out in the annals of Canadian mining.

And in the midst of this pell-mell rush, Sandon was born. It was an exciting town; brash and boisterous and down its crooked streets came a curious medley of humanity - the tinhorns, drifters, parsons, promoters, outlaws and prostitutes and Sandon took them in its stride for this was their type of town.

By 1898, Sandon was an incorporated city with a population pushing 2,000. The business section was the envy of rival centers and it was the complete mining town with 23 hotels and saloons, mining brokers offices, general stores, restaurants and a multitude of other concerns including diverse establishments like the Bank of British Columbia, the newspaper called the SANDON PAYSTREAK and even an opera house. It was served by not one but two railroads; the Kaslo and Slocan and the Canadian Pacific.

Its main street ran wide open twenty-four hours a day, seven days a week and in the backrooms, fortunes were made and lost by the buying or selling of a claim or by the turn of a card in Stud Horse.

This is the Silversmith Mine in 1900. One of scores in the area then.

Part of Sandon today, showing the city hall of 1900 on the extreme left and the courthouse on the right. In the foreground is Carpenter Creek.

The Virginia stands abandoned and boarded up, the sole survivor of more than two dozen hotels and saloons in the city in its heyday.

It was an eccentric town, other towns didn't board over a creek and then use it as the main street, but Sandon did. The inhabitants of other towns didn't place poker chips instead of cash in the church collections on Sunday, but they did in Sandon, and the churches cashed them.

But Sandon, like other mining towns, had its share of disasters. When the entire city was burned to the ground in a great inferno on May 3, 1900 it was taken in stride and within a few weeks a new and better town stood where the old one had been and business had scarcely faltered in between.

Eventually, however, the great mines exhausted their magnificent ore bodies and although Sandon struggled on until the 1950's it was a hollow effort for it had passed its best days and when in 1955, Carpenter Creek went on the rampage and took most of the then standing town with it, it should have been expected, because anything Sandon did, it always did with style and its death was no exception.

Now, only half a dozen buildings survive on the old main street from that grand era; the city hall, the Virginia, a hardware store, the tiny courthouse and several other long vacant structures. So you will have to listen carefully to hear the footsteps from the past echoing down the old boardwalk and the whirr of the roulette wheel in the saloons because the city is no more, Sandon is a shattered town.

SILVER KING CAMP

In 1887, silver ore was found in place on Toad Mountain. Within a year numerous promising claims were staked and from them a great mine was developed - the renowned Silver King, owned by the Halls of Nelson.

Silver King camp on Toad Mountain near Nelson around 1900.

By 1898, it was the heaviest producer on the mountain and 190 miners were working its depths. For two decades the Silver Ling was the greatest shipper of silver ore to the Nelson smelter and around its workings grew the camp which came to be known as Silver King Camp.

Eventually a sweeping forest fire destroyed the camp and now there is little to indicate that this notable camp ever existed in the area.

SILVERTON

Three miles south of New Denver is Silverton. It was, as its name implies, founded in the silver years, but it takes a little imagination now to visualize the main street as it once was, when hotels like the Lake View, Thistle and Thorburn House greeted the passerby and Mathieson's newspaper, the SILVERTONIAN, allowed him to catch up on local mining news or international events. Those were the years when the Galena Farm, Van Roi, Noonday and Standard were steady producers and times were good.

Now, most of the mining era structures have fallen to the wrecking crews and there is little left to remind the stranger that Silverton was once a noted mining town.

One of the few building from the mining years which is still standing in Silverton in the Slocan country.

SLOCAN CITY

It's known as Slocan now but there was a day when it was known far and wide as "Slocan City," and city it was.

You could pass by today but you wouldn't have in the 1890's when the

Slocan City in 1897. Notice the sacked silver ore on the dock.

A few souvenirs from the past from under the boardwalk in Slocan City.

The old General Store at Perry Creek Siding in the Slocan valley.

Some representative bottles from the Slocan City area.

town was roaring. It was the end of steel then and it was a rarity; sixteen hotels and saloons and dozens of stores on its one wide main street. At the north end, the dock, where the sternwheelers waited impatiently for cargo and passengers bound for New Denver, Three Forks, Sandon or other points north.

More than a few travelers who elected to hold over at the Victoria, International, Two Friends, Wilson or their choice of a dozen other hotels in the city in that era, lived to regret it,for they often got no farther: the gamblers of Slocan City were notorious for their ability to separate strangers from their bankrolls and miners from their stakes. It was that kind of town and remained so until it lapsed in the second decade of this century.

Unfortunately, although half a dozen grand hotels remained until twenty years ago, not one of them has survived and even the dwellings of that era are almost non-existent in the town today. So, Slocan City lives on only in the photographs of the past. It deserved a better fate.

THREE FORKS

Its tenure was brief but in its day, Three Forks was a thriving town. Strategically located at the forks of three creeks: Carpenter, Seaton and Kane, it came on the scene in 1892, on the heels of the great silver finds of that era. When the Nakusp and Slocan Railway reached the forks in 1894,

A rare photograph of Three Forks. This is how the town looked on September 28, 1894. Sandon lay three miles beyond and farther up the draw.

it was already firmly established as a center and although it was razed by a forest fire that summer, such was the confidence in its future that it was rapidly rebuilt.

By 1897, Henderson's Gazeteer listed fifteen businesses in the town and the weary traveler of that day could choose from fully half a dozen hotels: the Brunswick, Black's, Richelieu, Wilmington, Slocan or Miner's Exchange. On its streets, Madigan's stages with twice daily connections to Cody and Sandon, and the pack trains of G.B. Matthews lent a colourful touch to this frontier town.

The pinnacle of activity was undoubtedly from 1892 to 1902, for by 1909, the town had passed its peak and as nearby Sandon gained prominence, it gradually faded from view.

Now old Three Forks is a decimated site, with little meeting the eye to indicate that it was a center of considerable importance three quarters of a century ago. And the three creeks still flow unaltered and unaware that the town they once called Three Forks has passed on.

Below the townsite of Three Forks today. Remains of the railway bridges and debris from the past are about all that are left.

TROUT LAKE CITY

Where Lardeau Creek flows into the head of Trout Lake is a logical site and on it once stood Trout Lake City. It came to life in the same era as Camborne and its rival, Ferguson. It was the practical way point for the upper Lardeau country and when that district prospered, so did Trout Lake City.

In its best years, the Hume & Co. General Store, the Windsor Hotel, the Trout Lake TOPIC and half a dozen other enterprises were considered going concerns and the area was looked upon as "sure fire" country.

But the mining eventually died and so did Trout Lake City. Now, only the old hotel, a few crumbling log cabins and the forlorn cemetery remain from those years. Trout Lake City is less than a shadow.

Trout Lake City in 1904.

YMIR

When the placer miners of the 1860's followed the Salmo river north, looking for new gold creeks, they discovered that several streams yielded moderately good returns. One of these was Quartz Creek, a stream which empties into the Salmo river from the west. Near the mouth of this creek, a crude settlement known as Quartz Creek grew up.

In 1897, D.C. Corbin, the American railroad promoter, renamed the community Ymir, a name which had originally been used by the renowned surveyor G.M. Dawson, for the mountains nearby. And in that same era, an extensive mineral zone was found in the vicinity. Soon properties like the Queen, Yankee Girl, Dundee, Kootenay Belle, Ymir and many others came into production. The profits from these gold mines were high and Ymir grew. Soon sumptious hotels like the Palace and the Ymir vied for the steadily increasing trade and by 1899 an impressive two street town with an extensive business section stood on the flats.

The Palace and St. Charles hotels in Ymir in 1970.

The Pioneer Stables in old Ymir today.

Ymir was a bona fide mining town with all the faults and attributes of other mining towns but it lasted far longer than most of them and it was the late 1930's before its final and gradual decline set in.

Today, there are still sections of this town which are remarkably well preserved. Some mining towns seem to lose that special character over the years but Ymir has retained it - a walk through its streets will attest to that; characters like "Pete the Packer" are long gone but the magnificent Palace Hotel is still there and so is the stately St. Charles, which even in their twilight years seem to possess that intangible air, an air which still hovers in this town called Ymir.

The Ymir Hotel as it looked in 1910. This hotel is still in use in Ymir today.

ZINCTON

The ore body which built this camp was originally discovered in 1892. Although it was a massive vein, the ore was predominently zinc which at that time was a despised and unwanted metal. Thus, by 1895, only 110 tons of ore were shipped out and treated at the old smelter at Pilot Bay.

By 1903, G.W. Hughes had taken over control of the Lucky Jim Group, in anticipation of discovering ore with a higher silver content. On the strength of this theory, a camp was built which totally destroyed in the huge forest fire of 1910 which swept over the entire area.

In 1927, the Victoria Syndicate had acquired the claims and went into production and both a camp and a concentrator were erected in that year. For some years after Zincton held the position as one of the largest zinc producers in the Slocan until its ore body was finally depleted nearly two decades ago.

Today Zincton stands abandoned, with the camp and the concentrator slowly falling victim to the harsh winters and the salvagers. So Zincton, like so many others before, faces extinction; the inevitable sentence of mining towns.

Zincton as it looks today. It will probably not survive another decade of Slocan winters and then it too will vanish like so many other camps before it.

The abandoned Kaslo and Slocan Railway line.

GOLD CREEKS

● Erie Creek - This placer stream was probably discovered in the mid 1860's although its precise date of discovery has never been officially recorded. Once known as the North Fork, this stream which flows into the Salmo river was mined heavily in the canyon area with some coarse gold and nuggets up to the $6 size being taken out. Much of the gold was found on a clay hardpan. Prospects: an old gold creek with coarse gold in place is always worth investigating although possibilities are limited on this creek because the earlier work was generally extensive.

● Forty Nine Creek - This stream flows north from the Bonnington Range into the Kootenay river. Reputedly found in the late 1860's, it has been a fine gold stream with nuggets above the $1.50 size rather rare. Some hydraulicking was done with indifferent results, and drifting, ground-sluicing and other methods of recovery have also been used. As late as the 1930's, syndicates like the Black Watch were still at work on this creek. Prospects: Not encouraging. Forty Nine was never a bonanza creek and it is unlikely to turn into one at this late date.

Forty Nine Creek today with the signs of placer operations still visible along the creek. In the center of the photograph are the remains of an old sluice-box and in the immediate area shafts, water intakes, cribbing and other indications of the placer mining era remain.

● Kaslo River - Some early placering was done on this river which flows into Kootenay Lake near the town of Kaslo. Evidently discovered in the early 1880's, some fairly rough and coarse grained gold was taken out in the section from the powerhouse down to the river's mouth. It was worked by both whites and Chinese although large boulders in the stream made mining difficult. Its placer history was short. Prospects: limited, the placer ground does not extend upriver any great distance. There are many better placer rivers in the West Kootenay.

● Lardeau Creek - Placer gold was discovered on this creek prior to 1900. Lardeau Creek runs into the head of Trout Lake and has been mined since its discovery. Some relatively coarse gold had been found from time to time with the best ground near the locality known as Ten Mile which is at the junction of Gainer Creek with the Lardeau. This stream has been worked by several methods including hydraulicking. Prospects: somewhat better than many other Kootenay creeks because of its general inaccessibility to hobby miners.

An early photograph showing hydraulicking operations at Ten Mile on Lardeau Creek.

● Pend d' Oreille River - This noted placer river was probably discovered in 1856 when a quantity of gold dust was transported to Victoria. Placer gold was recovered along the full length of the river although the best ground was possibly at the mouth of the Salmo river. Both bars and some benches yielded and although much of the gold was coarse, nuggets above the ½ ounce size were seldom recovered. For decades this treacherous river was worked by miners; from their hydraulic operations at its mouth near Waneta, right up to the U.S. line. There are still a number of old, ruined prospectors cabins at various points along the river from those days and even now work is being done occasionally. Prospects: a dangerous river to work even under the best of conditions and because of hydro projects on the river, the miner is therefore limited to specific sections.

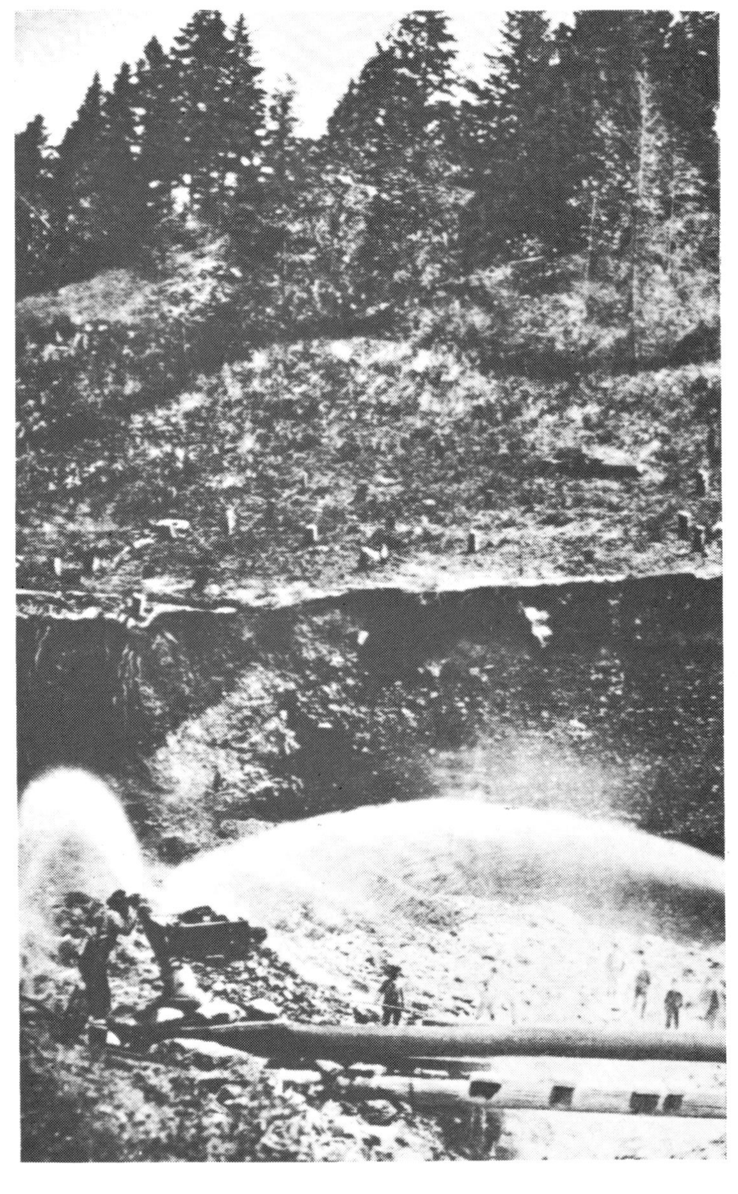

This old photograph shows a hydraulic operation close to Waneta, B.C. at the mouth of the Pend d'Oreille.

● Quartz Creek – This short stream empties into the Salmo river near Ymir and was known as a placer creek in the 1860's. It and several other creeks in the immediate area were gold producers although it was not noted as a nugget stream, the gold usually being fine. Prospects: With a total length of only two miles Quartz Creek cannot offer much to the prospector.

● Rover Creek – Another placer creek, west of Forty Nine Creek, which also emptied into the Kootenay River. Again, like its neighbour, it is primarily a fine gold creek although a little coarse gold has been found on occasion. Worked in a desultory fashion for many years, this creek has never been spectacular and doesn't indicate that it ever will be. It has generally been considered to be a mediocre creek at best. Prospects: it is unlikely that any length of good paying ground will be found on this stream although occasional sections could prove out.

● Salmo River - Originally known as the Salmon it was the richest of the Pend d'Oreille's tributaries and flows into that river from the north. The Salmo was a gold producer for most of its length and with a number of feeder placer gold creeks like Hall, Erie, Quartz and half a dozen others it offered good pay in a number of areas. The best placer ground found on the Salmo was from its mouth upriver for about four miles. This region was the richest a century ago and undoubtedly still is although the river runs swift and narrow in places which makes mining difficult. Prospects: Fairly encouraging. A lot of river to prospect with the possibilities of ancient channels. Undiscovered paystreaks could still exist on this gold river.

Miner's cabin along the Pend d'Oreille.

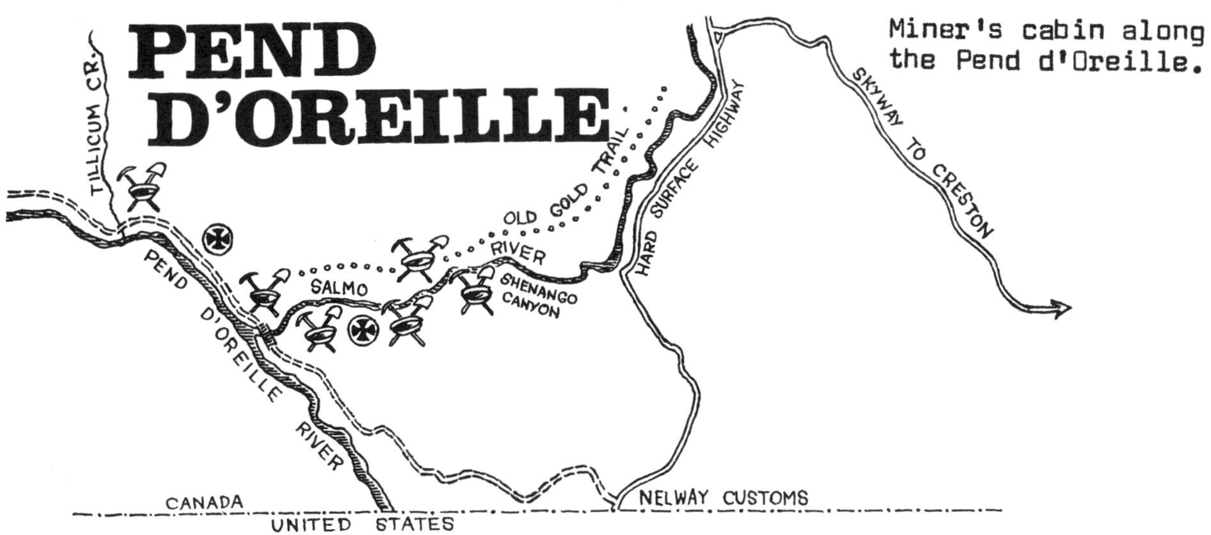

INDIAN COUNTRY

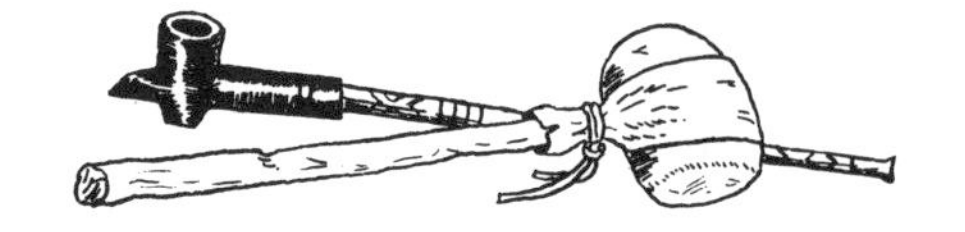

When the white placer miners flooded into the valleys of the West Kootenay in their quest for gold in the 1860's, they found the area almost uninhabited. The Indians, except in a few isolated instances, had vanished. There is considerable evidence that a plague had decimated the native population; in some cases completely depopulating villages and regions.

Actually, the region had been fairly heavily settled, especially along the great salmon rivers like the Kootenay and Slocan. James Teit, in his "Salishan Tribes of the Western Plateau," mentions somewhat more than twenty major habitation sites in the West Kootenay.

The Arrow Lakes were an especially attractive area then and there were a number of important villages in that region, amongst them: Nkema'-peleks, a berrying, fishing and root digging center at the head of the bight on the Upper Arrow Lake near the mouth of the Incomappleux River. There were also other villages along the lovely Arrows such as: Kospi'tsa, which meant "buffalo robe," and was located where Arrowhead was first founded. Others included Ku'sxena'ks, above Nakusp; Neqo'sp, now Nakusp, and Tci'uken, a hunting center just below Nakusp. There were two centers near Burton City also; Snexai'tsketsem and Xaie'ken. Unfortunately, most of these sites will be inundated by rising flood waters from the dam on

A few artifacts from the M.F. Edwards Collection in Trail. These are typical Kootenay River Indian artifacts and were recovered on that river.

the Lower Arrow Lake.

One of the most frequented localities was at the confluence of the Columbia and Kootenay Rivers. On the flat benches on the north side of the latter river there was a noted trading center known as Qepi'tles. A number of representative artifacts have been found in that region down through the years and even after the turn of the century, ancient burials were visible in the area. North of Qepi'tles there were also several village sites, including one on Waldie's Island where the kekuli depressions are still visible in the heavy undergrowth.

Although many of the sites are now flooded, once there was a great number of villages along the Kootenay River for it was a great river for fish; salmon below Bonnington Falls and Redfish above it. The West Arm, between Balfour and Nelson is one section of the river which has changed but little over the past century and even today artifacts are recovered in this area which were lost or misplaced those many years ago.

The Slocan River, however, was undoubtedly the best salmon river in the entire West Kootenay and although Teit only mentions three principal villages along that river, there were at least fourteen and perhaps more. The majority of these villages ranged from six to twenty kekulis close to the river bank and most of them were located between Slocan City and the junction of the Slocan River with Koch Creek.

An ancient Indian village once stood on this island near Castlegar which is known as Waldie's Island. There are still kekuli depressions on this island which was a favourite duck hunting area in the years when the Indians were masters of the land.

Thus the Lakes Indians traversed most of the West Kootenay, from the sandy wastelands of Fort Shepherd, along the perilous trails of the Pend d' Oreille, to the head and beyond the Kootenay and Arrow Lakes. Now they are gone from their ancient haunts and many of their sites have been long flooded and destroyed and only too few meticulously fashioned and once highly coveted artifacts remain to honour their passing.

Perforated net weights discovered in a cache at Harrop near Nelson. The largest weighed 14 pounds and the smallest about 5 pounds.

Some beautiful burial artifacts found in a blown out Indian burial along the Slocan River in 1932. Included are a ten inch ceremonial knife, a jade adze, a shell necklace with centerpiece, the rusted blade of a trade knife, two finely chipped knives and a large hunting arrowpoint.

The placer gold camp sometimes known as Kootenay in the year 1883, this was one of several boom towns along the once famous Wild Horse creek region in the East Kootenay.

THE EAST KOOTENAY

BRASS TRADE KETTLE OR BUCKET ~

INTRODUCTION

The East Kootenay - Wild Horse, Old Town, Bull River, Tobacco Plains, St. Eugene, North Star. Even the names have a special ring to them in this corner of the province.

It's a different country, this end of the Dewdney Trail; from dreary Corbin to deserted Wild Horse, from restored Fort Steele to forgotten Fort Kootenay, from the high Rockies to the rolling grasslands of the Tobacco Plains country.

This was the land of giants like Father Coccola, Isadore, chief of all the Kootenay Indians, Joe Bourgeois, the mine finder and an endless procession of prospectors, railroaders, fur men, river pilots, North West Mounted Police and a host of others who left their mark on this East Kootenay Country - the land of the "Chikamin" stone.

GHOST TOWNS

BULL RIVER

Although never as famous nor as colourful as its northern neighbour Wildhorse, Bull River also appeared in the 1860's when coarse placer gold was discovered below the canyon on a nearby river. Both the town and the river were later named after a prospector named Bull who had worked the placer ground along the river in that era.

When the gold-bearing gravels became exhausted after the turn of the century, lumbering and tie operations kept the little town alive and the doors of the Bull River Hotel and the general store open for a few more years.

Now a few false-front buildings; looking east to the old gold river and the scene of better days are all that remain from the early years - Bull River has been passed by.

Several buildings in Bull River today.

CORBIN

All the ghost towns of the west have their own peculiar atmosphere, but of these deserted towns, the gloomiest are the coal towns; and in the shadows of the Rockies one of the most eerie of these places still stands and Corbin is its name.

From 1908 to 1935, Corbin was the center of a huge strip mining operation on a surface lead known as the "Big Showing." At its height, the town counted a population of 600; it also had its own railway, the Eastern British Columbia, a large company store and a hotel appropriately named the Flathead Hotel.

Corbin, however, expired dramatically and abruptly when, in the spring of 1935, labour troubles between the Corbin Collieries and the local union erupted into violence which soon turned into a full-scale and bloody riot in which scores of special policemen, company officials and miners were injured before order was finally restored.

This was the end of the town, for shortly after, the Corbin Collieries closed down its operation and the town began to die. Although sporadic attempts were made to work the "Big Showing" profitably they were not successful and when the final venture in 1951 proved to be an economic failure, the town was abandoned.

Today, the decaying remnants of the town still stand on the original townsite in its spectacular natural setting but when you wander along the neglected railway line, past the vacant and staring houses and the leaning tipple, you invariably feel that there is something almost haunting about the town they call Corbin.

The crumbling coal tipple in Corbin, B.C., one of the last survivors of the Corbin Collieries operation along the "Big Showing" lead in the old coal town. Corbin, once boasting a population of 600, is now a forgotten ghost town in a secluded valley in the Rocky Mountains in the East Kootenay country of south-eastern British Columbia.

Corbin in 1909.

Several of the half dozen deserted buildings standing in Corbin today.

FORT STEELE

The most celebrated of all the historic towns in the East Kootenay is old Fort Steele.

Strangely, it wasn't even a mining town in a country full of mining towns and its beginning was hardly auspicious. It was first a fur trading post and then by the late 1860's, a river crossing known as Galbraith's Ferry, and so it remained for another twenty years until an odd twist of fate caused its sudden rise to prominence.

In 1884, two American prospectors were found murdered on the Golden Trail, shortly afterwards, two Kootenay Indians; Kapla and Isadore, were charged with the murders and a warrant was issued for their arrest. The two suspects were eventually apprehended and placed under heavy guard in the jail at Wild Horse. The Kootenay Indian chief, Isadore, who incidentally was not related to the accused Isadore, promptly forced the lock-up with some of his warriors and released the prisoners. Compounding this high-handed action, they then issued an ultimatum to several of the government officials in Wild Horse.

This precipitous act by the Kootenay Indian chief did not go unnoticed and by the spring of 1887, 75 men and two officers of D Troop of the North West Mounted Police left Fort Macleod for the Wild Horse district under the command of the resolute Supt. Sam Steele.

Arriving at Galbraith's Ferry in late July after a difficult trip, Steele quickly arranged with R. Galbraith to purchase ten acres of land on high ground on the bench for the erection of a fort. The chosen fort site was strategically located at the confluence of the Kootenay River and Wild Horse Creek and it was a natural crossroads, for at that spot, the Dewdney, Wild Horse, Sand Point, Kalispell and Findlay Trails all merged. So, the North West Mounted Police built their barracks and Fort Steele came into being.

One of the first houses to be erected in Fort Steele. The Kootenay River may be seen in the background to the right. Circa 1889.

With four members fewer than the year before, the North West Mounted Police leave Fort Steele in 1888 bound for Fort Macleod in the N.W.T.

Looking down Riverside Avenue in Fort Steele in 1898. The old North West Mounted Police jail is in the right foreground while the main part of the town is in the background.

The water tower in the old and unrestored part of Fort Steele.

Historic marker overlooking the Kootenay River south of Fort Steele.

The Indian troubles subsided and the N.W.M.P. left the Kootenay in 1888 to return to Fort Macleod in the North West Territories.

From 1888 to 1891, there was little activity in the region except along the Wild Horse where the hardy placer miners continued to work the golden gravels. But in the fall of 1892, Joe Bourgeois, of Red Mountain and Rossland fame, stumbled across a fabulously rich showing of silver-lead ore nearby and the celebrated North Star Mine leapt to fame.

With this discovery, Fort Steele suddenly became the focal point of hundreds and then thousands of miners as they flowed across the line to seek their Eldorados.

In that same year the first riverboat, the Annerly, made the first run from Jennings, Montana to the Fort. And as the North Star went into production, Fort Steele boomed, North Star Landing wasn't a townsite but the former was; lots sold at inflated prices to eager bidders, hotels like the Steele, Delgardno's, Mountain House, International, Coeur d' Alene and others lined busy Riverside Avenue and Keep's Bank, Grace's newspaper, THE PROSPECTOR and a myriad of other concerns gave the town an exclusive air.

As the decade progressed as increasing number of sternwheelers began to ply the dangerous stretch of river between Jennings and Fort Steele, as the Ruth, Gwendoline, North Star, J.D. Farrell and Rustler competed for the mounting trade. Skilled and iron-nerved riverboat captains like Armstrong and Miller needed all their experience to avert disaster along the river and their skills gave rise to the memorable phrase; "Give a Kootenay pilot a heavy dew and his boat will arrive on schedule." The riverboats didn't always arrive on schedule but they continued to arrive and as they did, Fort Steele profited.

And the Fort continued to grow and prosper antil fate played her final joker. In 1898, the Crowsnest Pass Railway was fully expected to run to Fort Steele, but when the steel was laid it went instead to upstart Cranbrook some nine miles to the south-west. Fort Steele had been bypassed. This staggering blow was followed closely by another when in the fall of

Looking south on Riverside Avenue in Fort Steele in the year 1898.

that year when two sternwheelers were wrecked in "the elbow" of Jennings Canyon. The North Star ore was then diverted to the Trail smelter and the riverboat business, which had been the life-blood of Fort Steele, was no longer needed.

It was the end of Fort Steele and its doom was officially sealed when the government offices were moved to Cranbrook in 1904. From that day on the Fort was a dying town. Through the decades it became more and more of a ghost town until it was finally restored by the provincial government several years ago.

Now Fort Steele stands again but perhaps it has lost something in the transformation - the mood seems to have changed in the restored town although it has remained the same in the old part of town by the original watertower, that part which still overlooks the historic trails of those gold seekers of yesterday.

KOOTENAI OR WILDHORSE

It's possible to walk down the main street of Kootenay today and yet never realize that it was ever a street. There are a few clues, however, which give it away; stone steps leading to vacant sites, burned timber and debris in an overgrown clearing, broken bottles and a few stray coins scattered amongst the ashes.

And it was a town once - about ninety years ago, when the Wild Horse was still the big gold creek in the East Kootenay. A thousand miners had pushed up the narrow canyon then to stake claims along the banks of the Wild Horse, and after, they took time out to build a town which was called Fisherville. But that camp didn't last long when it was discovered that

Celebrations at the post office of the mining camp called Kootenai on the Wild Horse in 1883.

The main street of Kootenai in 1883.

A few square nails and old coins found along the street.

Seven of hundreds of Chinese pottery items recovered from the Wild Horse area. These items are from the Dempsey Collection of Fort Steele.

One of a dozen cabins still standing along the Wild Horse near Kootenai.

gold lay under the townsite, so Fisherville was simply dismantled by the prospectors in order to work the ground underneath. A new camp came into being soon after, a camp south of and higher than Fisherville had been. This new mining camp was named Kootenai although it often went by the name of Wild Horse.

Kootenai stood for years, a monument to the placer era long after Kee Chin, Dave Griffiths and a host of others had laid away their gold pans and Wild Horse had ceased to be famous.

Finally, it too fell victim to fire, vandals and time, and of old Kootenai only a few charred relics of its past remain. But down by the river they continue to call the Wild Horse, and in the canyon nearby, the magic of those indelible years stays on.

LUMBERTON

Today Lumberton is completely abandoned, the stark cement walls of its mill rising above the ruins and foundations of long dismantled homes.

It was once known as Watts or Wattsburg after A.E. Watts. Those were the years after the turn of the century when Watts, the founder and owner of the lumber mill, literally ran the town. Later, when he sold out to the gigantic B.C. Spruce Mills Ltd., they installed one of the most up-to-date mills in the province and Lumberton was on the map with a population of 225, a post office and a general store to serve the three dozen company houses on the townsite.

Eventually, the hills nearby became barren of timber and Lumberton was closed down by the company. That was more than thirty years ago and Lumberton has remained neglected and deserted to this day.

The ruins of Lumberton in 1970.

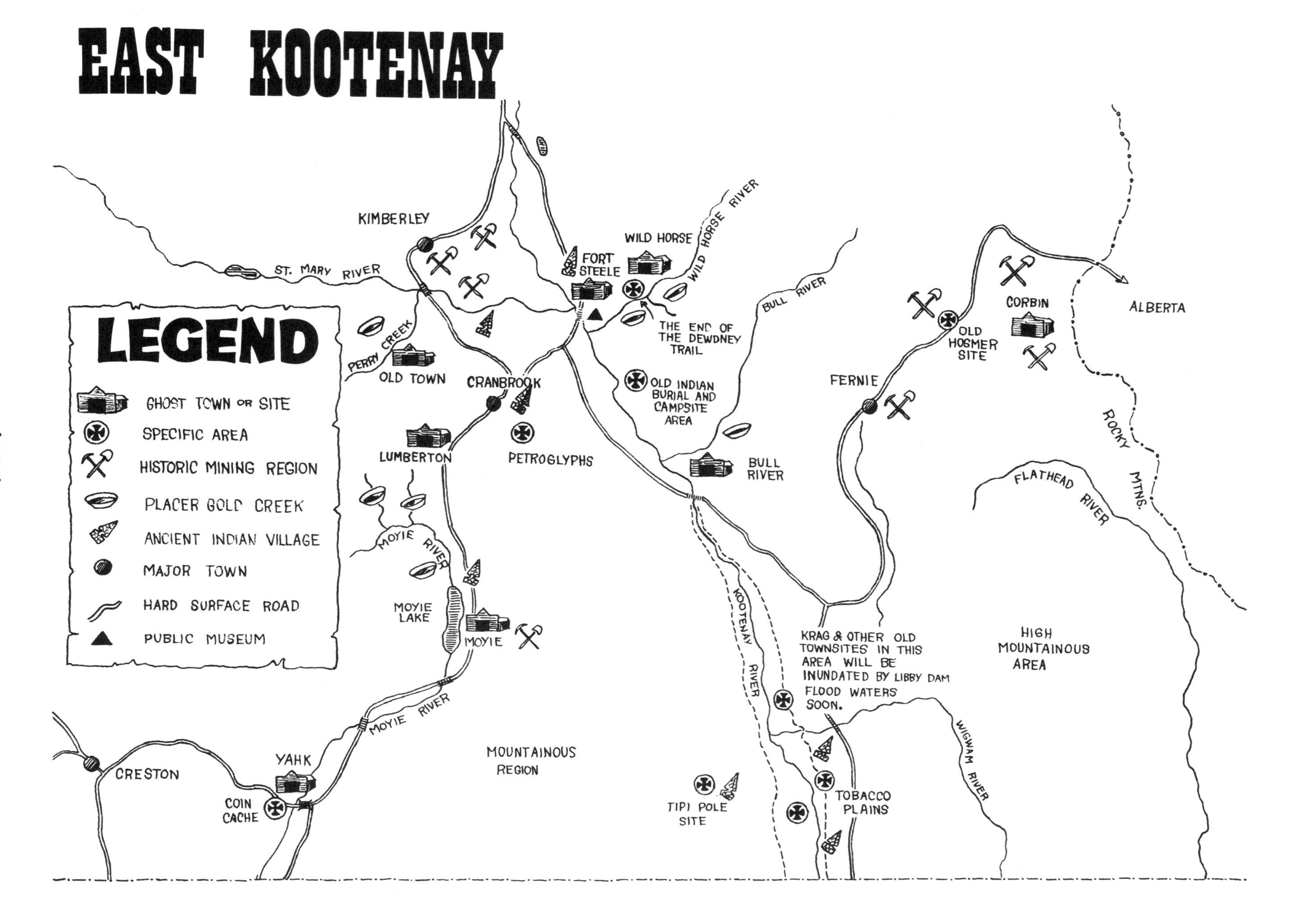
EAST KOOTENAY
LEGEND
GHOST TOWN OR SITE
SPECIFIC AREA
HISTORIC MINING REGION
PLACER GOLD CREEK
ANCIENT INDIAN VILLAGE
MAJOR TOWN
HARD SURFACE ROAD
PUBLIC MUSEUM
KIMBERLEY
ST. MARY RIVER
PERRY CREEK
OLD TOWN
CRANBROOK
LUMBERTON
PETROGLYPHS
FORT STEELE
WILD HORSE
WILD HORSE RIVER
THE END OF THE DEWDNEY TRAIL
OLD INDIAN BURIAL AND CAMPSITE AREA
BULL RIVER
BULL RIVER
MOYIE RIVER
MOYIE LAKE
MOYIE
MOYIE RIVER
MOUNTAINOUS REGION
CRESTON
YAHK
COIN CACHE
TIPI POLE SITE
KOOTENAY RIVER
KRAG & OTHER OLD TOWNSITES IN THIS AREA WILL BE INUNDATED BY LIBBY DAM FLOOD WATERS SOON.
TOBACCO PLAINS
WIGWAM RIVER
FERNIE
OLD HOSMER SITE
CORBIN
ALBERTA
ROCKY MTNS.
FLATHEAD RIVER
HIGH MOUNTAINOUS AREA

MOYIE

The sleepy appearance of this little town is deceptive because Moyie has a background few towns can lay claim to.

In the 1890's, with prospectors roaming all through the hills and draws of the East Kootenay some great mines were discovered; the famous North Star in 1892, and the incomparable Sullivan in the same year. But the Moyie Lake country was somehow missed and it fell to a Kootenay Indian to locate a mine which for years was the leading silver-lead producer in British Columbia - and the mine was called the St. Eugene.

In that mining era, a dedicated and many-sided Roman Catholic priest, Father Nicholas Coccola, mission priest to the Kootenay Indians informed his flock that he should be told if any of them came across a rock which they called "chikamin." Chikamin was stone or ore with visible metal in it. If they happened to find a good vein of it, the priest continued, any proceeds realized from it would be used to build a new and badly needed mission church.

Several months later, Father Coccola received a visitor, an Indian who had once been the priest's most virulent enemy but who had been won over later and had become a firm friend of the priest's. The Indian's name was Pierre and in his hands he held several samples of ore, which, he stated he had obtained from an entire mountain made out of chikamin.

Coccola, alert to the possibilities of a new find, carefully examined

The old firehall in Moyie today, complete with ancient fire reels, hose, buckets and bell.

Part of the mining town of Moyie about 1902.

The St. Eugene Mine about the same time.

Historic marker by the highway in Moyie.

Moyie's original firehall and bell tower with the bell still in place. Next door, a tiny false front store leans precariously. Moyie - 1970.

the samples and still interested, took them to James Cronin, a railroad and mining man in the. Cronin looked them over slowly then pronounced them to be high grade galena ore.

The determined priest then went to Fort Steele where he obtained a free miner's licence and then he and Cronin, guided by Pierre, set out to find the outcrop. Their journey took them south-west of Fort Steele where they then followed a river which eventually took them to a mountain lake, skirting the cliffs on the southern side they edged their way toward the south-west corner. Finally the Indian stopped and pointed to a ledge above them. "There is the chikamin place." he said. Quickly scrambling up the steep hillside, the priest and the promoter stopped at the top and gazed in wonder - for before their amazed eyes was a vein of practically solid galena, and it was almost four feet wide. Two claims were staked then and there; one was called the St. Eugene, after Father Coccola's mission and the other was called the Peter. From them were born the great St. Eugene Mine and the town of Moyie.

And so Father Coccola got his new church, Pierre got a new house, and Cronin became a mining millionaire.

In time the mine became the representative silver-lead mine of the East Kootenay and yielded well over 1,000,000 tons of silver-lead ore in its lifetime. Moyie grew too, by 1901 to a population of 845, with a post office, a newspaper optimistically named the MOYIE LEADER, three hotels, four stores and several other enterprises.

Both the mine and the town have been idle for years now, but when one wanders through its byways the years do not seem long gone: Father Coccola's church still stands on a back street, the original firehall and its bell tower are there yet, the workings of the mighty St. Eugene loom over the town as they did then and on the outskirts, the little cemetery, with its scores of overgrown tombstones give silent testimony that this was the town and there was a day when it was proudly called Moyie City.

Moyie after the C.P.R. had laid its line into the mining town.

OLD TOWN

When Perry Creek was second only to the Wild Horse in the placer gold years, the camp that harboured the miners was called Old Town, a town with dance halls, several saloons and hotels, three stores and even a jail.

Perry Creek went well for ten years and Old Town went well for the same length of time but when the gold creek declined so did the town. It is a ravaged site today, only one of the original buildings remains and it verges on collapse - when it goes, so will the place called Old Town.

The last of the original buildings in Old Town on Perry Creek. It has been stated that it is the remains of an aged H.B.Co. post but the records of the company do not support this claim. It was probably a free trader's.

YAHK

Half a century ago Yahk had a population bordering on 400 and its hotels were hard pressed to keep up with the business; a lumber town was a good town and Yahk was a lumber town. But fortune is a fleeting thing and by 1930, the town was dying, its population a fraction of what it was at its height. Certain towns, however, never realize that they are fading and they decline to accept their fate.

Today, although time has bypassed Yahk, the old hotels still front on the main street of yesterday while across the tracks, the traffic moves by on the highway of today - oblivious to the fact that old Yahk is still waiting for those flourishing days which will never return.

One of the hotels on the old main street in Yahk today.

A cache of silver dollars, dimes, quarters and fifty cent pieces found in old Yahk in 1970. This treasure trove is now in the collection of Al Watt of Creston.

GOLD CREEKS

● Bull River - This tributary of the Kootenay River flows into that river from the east near Cranbrook. Discovered in 1864, the Bull River was a good placer river with a reputation for coarse gold. The 1898 mining report stated: "The Old Pack Bridge was a centre of activity on the Bull River in the early 60's, when the discovery of gold placers, a mile above and below the bridge, made the river famous and returned small fortunes to many prospectors." The pay dirt on this river was confined to a limited stretch of the river and the origin of the gold was a mystery. Prospects: Hydro development has virtually ruined this river for placer mining. One or two places are conducive to sniping but otherwise not good.

The turbulent Bull River below the Old Pack Bridge in 1898.

● Boulder Creek - This creek joins the Wild Horse from the south. It was a relatively good placer stream especially near its mouth. Worked by both Chinese and whites, a considerable amount of coarse, rough edged gold was taken out. It has been worked to bedrock in places. Prospects: any of the feeder gold creeks of Wild Horse were excellent placer creeks, but like the Wild Horse they have been thoroughly prospected by experienced miners who didn't miss much.

● Findlay Creek - Discovered by a part-breed of that name in 1863 which caused a short-lived rush into the creek in that year. This stream flows into the Kootenay River from the western side just to the south of Canal Flats. In the early years a considerable amount of coarse gold with some good sized nuggets were obtained from generally shallow diggings. It was worked by both whites and Chinese for some time. Prospects: Findlay has been well worked and prospected although there are still a few selected places where snipers work. A generally spotty creek although colours are still found in several places along the creek.

● Moyie River - This river which lies south of Cranbrook was found in the late 1860's after the discovery of Wild Horse had brought placer miners into the area. It has produced gold in quantity in several places. One of the richest sections was just below the falls on the upper river, in the 1930's, McEwen and Oscarson took out a large amount of gold by tunneling. Placer gold was obtained right down to the shores of Moyie Lake and all along the river, ranging from coarse to quite fine. Prospects: a fairly interesting river with an intriguing history. Still a lot of potentially good ground to cover and the possibilities of discovering isolated pay-streaks even today cannot be completely dismissed.

The falls on the Moyie River today. It was a difficult section to work in the early years but the old-timers managed to recover some exceptionally good placer gold from this part of the canyon. Some workings as well as the original trail are still visible in this photograph.

One of the oldest cabins still standing on Perry Creek today. Inside the cabin is a water wheel completely hand-made with the "walking bar" still in place.

● Nigger Creek - This small stream runs into the Moyie on the upper part of that river. It was discovered in the same year as the Moyie and its other tributaries. Worked by both Chinese and whites it was not quite as productive as other placer creeks in the area but did yield a considerable amount of gold in the early years. Prospects: probably not as good as the Moyie. Possibilities for sniping and drifting as it has not been cleaned as well as some other more well known placer creeks in the area.

● Palmer Bar Creek - This creek, also a tributary of the Moyie, was found in the 1860's and was worked for several decades. Palmer Bar did give up a quantity of placer gold and was considered to be a better paying creek than either Weaver or Nigger the other two main tributaries of the Moyie River. Gold from this creek was generally fine with nuggets above the $3 size rather rare. Prospects: any tributary of the Moyie is worth looking at and Palmer Bar is no exception.

● Perry Creek - One of the best placer creeks in the East Kootenay. Perry creek was discovered by one Frank Perrier in 1867. Such was the size and quantity of placer gold on the creek that a rush immediately followed the discovery. This stream has a fascinating history with such places as the "jewellery box" a spot where the nuggets recovered were in a form shaped like a pendant. Although the mining records indicate that there was from

The steam shovel at work on upper Perry Creek in 1903. This operation proved to be a failure and the steam shovel stands today by the creek.

The Falls of Perry Creek. This was the most productive of all the placer gold spots on the creek. Note the old placer workings at the side of the falls.

eight to ten miles of paying creek, the good section was only about five miles long. Rich from surface to bedrock with the latter being very rich in places. Peculiarities on the creek were many; quicksand in the flats area; only one of its many tributaries carried gold and the gold always occurred where the heavy, black ironstone was encountered. This creek was worked by various methods; tunneling, hydraulicking, steam shovel, wing-damming, sniping and so on including shafts to a depth of 70 feet or more. Prospects: Perry Creek is a most interesting creek. Gold is still being recovered in various sections with the falls area considered the best. A number of methods are successful in varying degrees, even the panner and the sniper have places where they find interesting ground. This creek is worth investigating.

The Perry Creek water wheel on its original site. This undershot wheel is now at Fort Steele although there are two other wheels still standing farther up this gold creek.

● Weaver Creek - Discovered when the Moyie River was found to carry placer gold. Weaver is also a tributary of the Moyie and along with Palmer Bar and Nigger it was worked for some decades. The gold is generally fine on this creek with good sized nuggets scarce. This creek also joins the Moyie above Moyie Lake. Prospects: there are still possibilities on this creek for the sniper and small operator although it has been well worked over the years. The early days were evidently fairly productive on this stream and occasional spots should remain.

● Wild Horse River - This river was originally called Stud Horse Creek and was discovered by American prospectors in the fall of 1863. One of the few placer streams flowing west from the Rockies to contain placer gold in quantity it empties into the Kootenay River near old Fort Steele. Its total output over its long life-span has been variously estimated at anywhere from $2,000,000 to $30,000,000 and although the true total will never be known for sure, it probably yielded close to $7,000,000 in gold and was destined to go down in history as one of the greatest gold creeks in the entire province. The stream was rich right from the surface gravel down to bedrock, much of the gold was coarse and rough-edged, and nuggets were plentiful. The largest ever taken out was by Mike Reynolds, a miner who worked the creek in the 1860's and that nugget weighed 36 ounces. It was a stream which was so rich that it was worked extensively; hydraulic operations, tunnels, shafts and every other conceivable method was used to recover the valuable metal. It went through two eras of great activity; the first era was from 1863 to 1868 and the second from 1885 to 1900. Some miners like Dave Griffith spent a lifetime on this creek and did well. Prospects: it is difficult to assess the prospects of this river, it was the richest in the whole of the southern interior and it yield was enormous, but it has been worked and re-worked by both Chinese and whites. No doubt there are areas along this creek which would still yield well, but it has been so well prospected that the chances of finding an area like this is rather slim. There are a few places where a sniper could obtain some fair returns but generally the chances must be considered only fair in spite of its renowned history.

Some the workings along the Wild Horse today.

Red Headed Davis's pack train, loaded with prospecting supplies, about to cross the Quesnel river in the late 1860s. (Archives photograph)

THE CARIBOO

This is the story of Antler Creek in the Cariboo. Although there were other placer creeks of more lasting fame and far richer, it was the discovery of gold in this stream in 1860 which touched off the greatest gold rush in the history of British Columbia.

ANTLER CREEK

After the initial frantic rush to the Fraser river in 1858 and the subsequent discovery of gold on bars like Hill's, Murderers, Sailors, Boston, China and scores of others, a vanguard of prospectors gradually worked upriver panning the bars and mining the benches as they went. Ever mindful of the original source of the gold, the elusive "motherlode," they pressed on. Lytton and Lillooet were established and then left behind as they continued northward; at Quesnellemouth they turned east, gleaning the incomparable metal as they followed the Quesnel. At the forks they found rich diggings and for months it became the centre of the mining activity, but when the quantity of gold decreased the quest continued. On the north fork of the river the trail of gold was lost at the falls, five miles below Cariboo Lake. Finally, in the spring of 1860, a rich placer creek was found flowing southeast into Cariboo Lake. In the discovery party was one "Doc" Keithley, a prospector who had washed out the first colours from the creek. In honour of this achievement the party named the stream after him. Within weeks the entire length of Keithley Creek was staked as newcomers flocked pell-mell to the new diggings.

Although it was the richest creek yet found, a number of prospectors felt that somewhere beyond Keithley even richer creeks awaited discovery. One of these miners was an American named John Rose. Rose had a strange magnetism, a certain aura which caused others to follow his lead. He was, many prospectors believed, a man of destiny.

Late that fall, Rose, accompanied by George Weaver, "Doc" Keithley and a Canadian named McDonald, set out from Keithley Creek in search of new ground. Carrying only a few days provisions they ascended that creek for about five miles and then veered north-eastward up a ravine. Reaching Snowshoe Creek, a tributary of Keithley, they followed it to its source some seven miles further. Finally they reached the summit of the watershed dividing the streams flowing into Cariboo Lake from those creeks flowing eastward, northward and westward into the Bear, Willow and Cottonwood Rivers.

For the first time the entire territory lay spread out before them; never before had prospectors viewed the panorama of the Cariboo. Over the whole region lay a mantle of silence and solitude, a wilderness untouched - it must have been an unforgettable experience. Far below them, flowing in a northerly direction, lay a creek. Although they had panned hundreds of streams in the past two years, each time they felt a familiar surge of excitement, a sense of anticipation. Would this one be the creek? Rose led the descent and several hours later they found themselves in a narrow valley; the stream wound through its centre and here and there bedrock protruded. Within minutes they were at work washing the gravels. A few moments passed before the results were visible, then they saw it - gold! The bottoms of their pans were covered with golden flakes and nuggets. It was unbelievable, it was a bonanza!

They were elated. Every panful was rich, one contained a staggering quarter of a pound of gold and even the leaner pans yielded enough metal to pay a day's wages. They slowly realized that they had stumbled across an Eldorado creek. The dream of a lifetime, and they had barely scratched its surface.

They panned feverishly until darkness fell, and then, in the light of a campfire they held a conference. They were the only miners in the Cariboo who knew that the creek existed but they were running precariously low on supplies. Two of them would have to return to Keithley Creek for provisions.

Early the following morning they awoke to find a foot of snow on the ground. Their plight was serious, the supplies would have to be obtained immediately. According to most sources Keithley and Weaver agreed to return for the provisions. Rose and McDonald were to hold the ground and build a log cabin while their partners were away. Both of the former were sworn to secrecy and vowed not to divulge any information to anyone about their discovery. Being old hands they knew that if word leaked out about their find the creek would be stampeded and staked from end to end. The next day, after an arduous journey, the two prospectors were on the outskirts

Keithley Creek's Chinatown in 1902. In this picture the old gold camp is shown in its decline after the hectic 1860s. (Archives photograph)

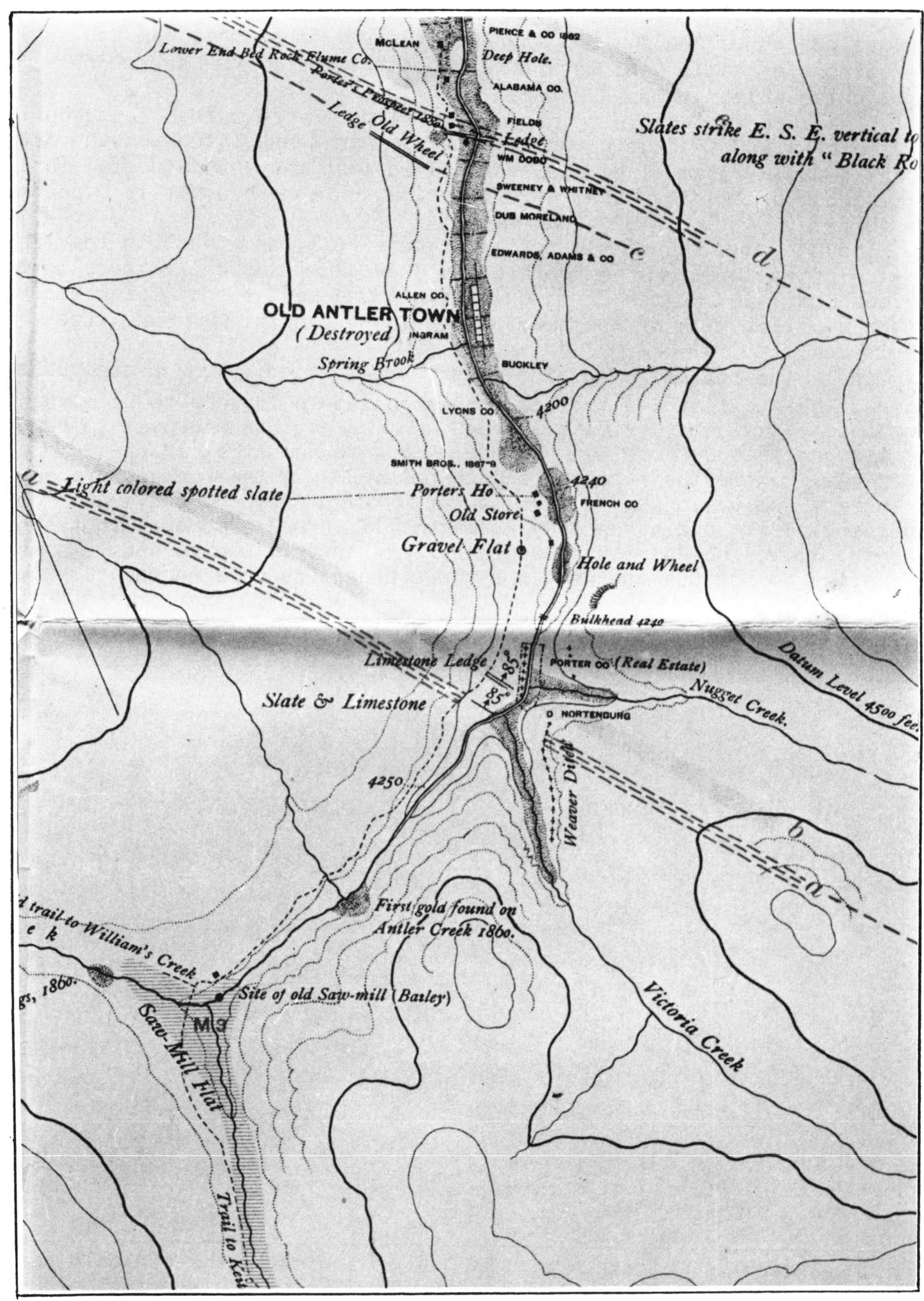

1885-86 Amos Bowman map of upper Antler Creek showing close detail of workings. Notice the Discovery claim. (Canada West Collection)

of Keithley Creek. After reminding each other about their pact of silence they made their way to "Red Headed" Davis's store. The proprietor and two or three miners were lounging inside. Nonchalently Keithley and Weaver ordered their supplies, hoping to remain as inconspicuous as possible. Strangely, although they were extremely careful, the other miners in the room somehow sensed that they were concealing something. No one will ever know exactly what happened to tip off the others although years later one of the miners who was present then said; "their mouths didn't say much but their eyes said a lot." As a result, by the time Keithley and Weaver had collected their provisions and left the premises scores of miners were waiting patiently outside, packed and ready to hit the trail. Realizing that their secret had leaked out, the two partners, not even bothering to try to dissuade the others took to the trail. Immediately a long string of prospectors swung into line behind them and together they trudged off silently through the new fallen snow. Thus began one the Cariboo's most unusual gold stampedes.

Needless to say, their arrival at Antler Creek the following day was greeted with some surprise when Rose and McDonald saw the horde of miners accompanying their partners. As the discovery claims had been staked by

This old photograph of the Fraser river shows the terrain encountered by the prospectors of 1858 as they made their way upriver in search of the fabled and often elusive motherlode.

the four discoverers, the new arrivals began to lay claim to other parts of the creek. However, as the ground was covered with more than a foot of snow, the prospectors were staking blind - a chancy business. Some, guided almost by instinct, chose ground which eventually proved incredibly rich. Others, often on adjoining claims, held ground which ultimately turned out to be virtually worthless. Few dreamt that they were poised on the edge

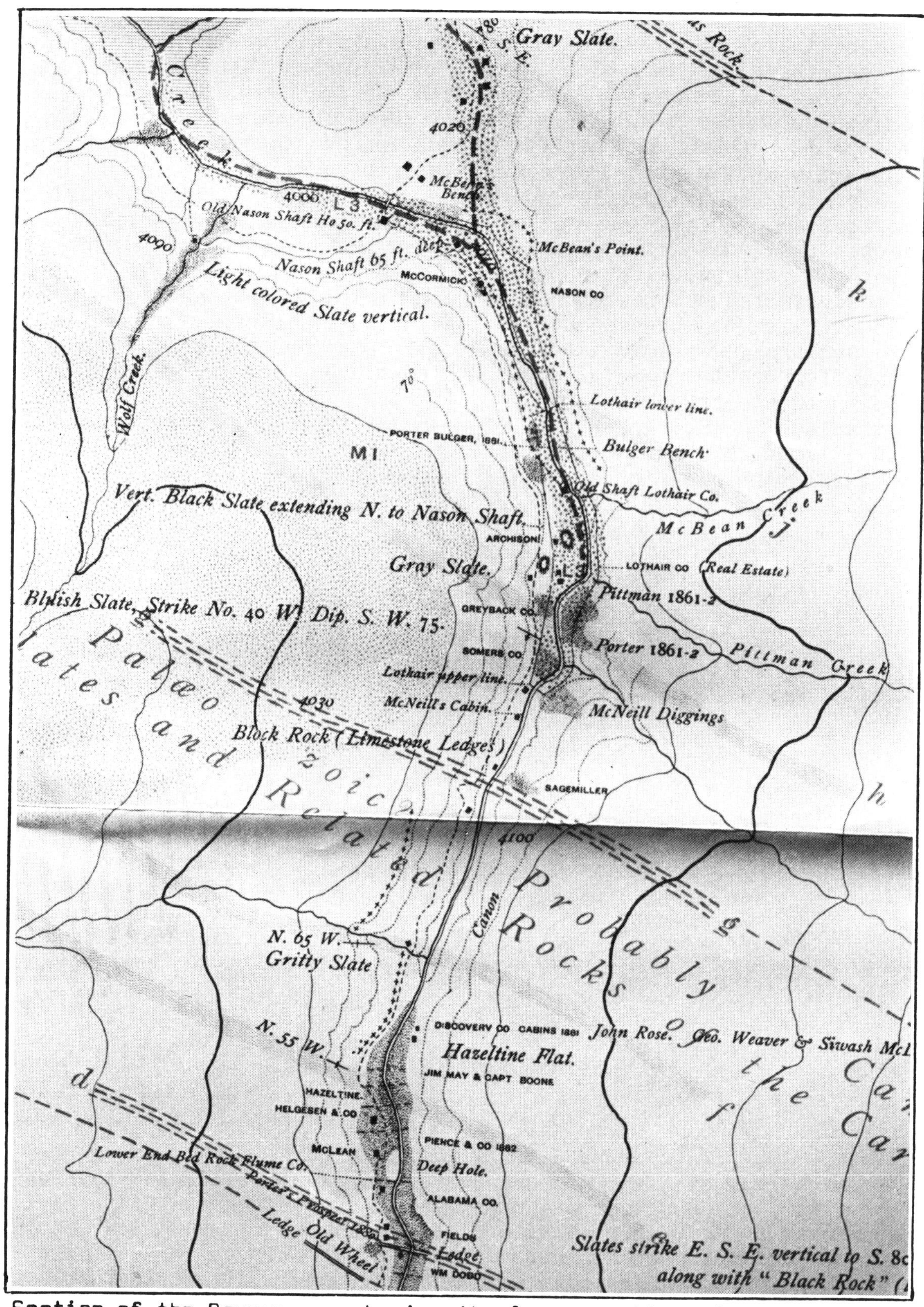

Section of the Bowman map showing the lower section of Antler Creek. The detail is exceptionally accurate. (Canada West Collection)

of the richest gold-field in British Columbia and that barely four miles away lay a stream which was soon to become the premier gold creek in the province, Williams Creek.

As winter settled in, the prospectors, determined to hold onto their claims, made the best of a deplorable situation. Rose and McDonald's cabin was the only permanent building on the creek, the remainder of the miners, according to Gold Commissioner Nind, who arrived in Antler Creek in March of 1861 to settle claims disputes, were holed up in the snow, which, by

A waterwheel of the early 1860s. There were scores of wheels along all of the major gold creeks in the Cariboo in those years.
(Archives photograph)

that time had reached an awesome depth of nearly seven feet. Although the living conditions were unbelievably harsh and food scarce, some of the miners had managed to work their claims by burrowing through the snow to ground level, then heating the earth with fires and digging down to the bedrock. The returns, in many cases, were startlingly good.

Surprisingly, although there were some heated disputes over rights to the same ground, there were no shootings or otherwise bloody frays which had been so prevalent along the lower Fraser only two years before. The men who had survived the arduous trek into the wilderness of the central part of the province were a far different breed from some of the riff-raff who had flocked to the Fraser river in 1858.

Even in the most remote wilderness the news of a strike always seems to spread. Undoubtedly, Rose, who had discovered Rose's Bar on the Yuba River in California in 1848, was partially responsible. Many prospectors were convinced that wherever Rose went, gold was always close at hand.

By the spring of 1861 the rush to Antler Creek had become a torrent. The miners soon found that the best section of the creek was the shallow part which extended for about 1½ miles along the stream below Sawmill Flats and above the canyon. Mainly from this productive section came a daily output of over $10,000. Some sections of the bedrock, according to Bancroft's works, yielded a staggering $1,000 in gold to the square foot. By today's prices this would be nearly $9,000 to the square foot - almost unbelievable.

As prospectors continued to pour into the region all the available ground on Antler was soon taken up. Some of the more adventurous miners, unable to obtain claims on the creek, began to fan out in an attempt to locate other gold creeks in the area. They were soon rewarded with success beyond their greatest expectations.

In quick succession Grouse and Wolfe creeks; California, Stevens and Beggs gulches, all tributaries of Antler and all gold bearing, were found. In the middle of February, William Cunningham, breaking into new territory, found the creek which still commemorates his name. From one crevice on the Discovery claim a total of fifty troy pounds of gold was extracted.

Gold fever mounted as news of these spectacular finds became known and prospecting parties began to strike out in every direction. By the early summer more new discoveries were reported. Lowhee Creek was found by the strange Richard Willoughby; Lightning was discovered by Jim Bell, Jack Hume and the doubly fortunate William Cunningham. And a creek to be known as Williams Creek, was found by a company of experienced old hands which included tough old Ed Stout, Michael Byrnes, Vital Laforce, Brown, Costello and William Dietz, who was better known as 'Dutch Bill,' who was accorded the honour of having the newly found creek named after him when he washed out the best pan of the day, a satisfying but not spectacular $1.25's worth of gold. But Williams Creek was only one of dozens of new placer creeks which were discovered in 1861. Prior to that date, the gold take had been measured in ounces, afterwards it was often calculated in pounds. And the wilderness was transformed as thousands of miners, drawn by the irresistable call of 'gold' came from all parts of North America and beyond. Soon the gold camps, Barkerville, Camerontown, Antler Town, Van Winkle, Richfield and dozens of others, roared to life. Along their muddy streets hard-eyed Californians brushed elbows with silent Chinese; green Englishmen competed with experienced Canadians, and over all the heady excitement of the gold-fields prevailed.

Although dwarfed by some of its more celebrated sisters, Antler, the original key to the Cariboo gold-fields, continued to produce steadily, and occasionally spectacularly. Hand mined in the 1860s and hydraulicked during the depressions of the 1890s and the 1930s, it yielded fortunes to many miners. Paradoxically, like so many of the locators of famous placer creeks in the Cariboo, the four original discoverers recovered little of its riches. "Doc" Keithley, George Weaver and "Siwash" McDonald slipped silently into obscurity. The fate of John Rose, the accepted leader of the original band, was even more bizarre. In the spring of 1863 he left Barkerville and headed north on a routine prospecting trip into the Bear river country. What happened remains a mystery, for John Rose, prospector non-pareil and woodsman complete, simply vanished, never to be seen from that day onwards.

GOLD ON THE INSIDE CHANNEL

Quesnel's Front Street in the 1890s, long after the high years of the Cariboo Gold Rush were over. The gold laden miners from the Tinker and the Prince of Wales claims tarried too long in the saloons along this rollicking street in 1863. (Vancouver City Archives photograph)

The turbulent and often treacherous waters of the Fraser River conceal an astonishing number of treasures, most of them lost during the early 1860s, that heyday of placer mining in British Columbia, an era before the famous Cariboo Road was completed when the Fraser was still the main highway from the central interior.

On rare occasions, a treasure story is backed by impressive and substantial documentary evidence. This is one such narrative, a tale about thirteen men; twelve miners and a French-Canadian steersman - and a massive hoard of lost gold.

I read the old newspaper account again. Two thousand troy ounces of gold! More than $800,000.00 worth at today's price. It had originally come from famous Williams Creek, during an era when that celebrated stream was El Dorado ground. Probably a fair proportion of the treasure had been in nugget form. If half of the lost gold was comprised of nuggets at least another twenty per cent could be added to the gold value, making a final total of $960,000.00. A significant amount by most standards.

It was, I was convinced, not only a legitimate treasure but also one of the most closely guarded secrets in British Columbia history. My notes also led me to believe that the bulk of this vast treasure still lay undisturbed along the bottom of a specific section of the Fraser River.

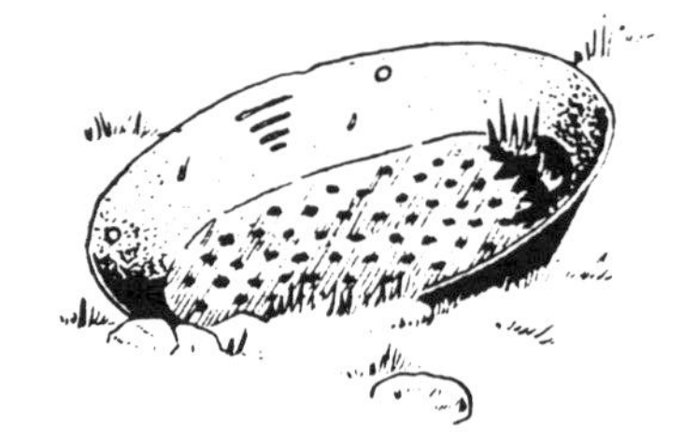

Once more I looked at the map lying on the table in front of me. For several minutes I peered intently at every bend and stretch in the river south of Quesnel. There were a number of islands downriver from that old town but none of them were even close to the location where the tragedy of 1863 had occurred.

I turned the details over in my mind. Logically the island mentioned in the original reports should have been on the map, somewhere between historic Rich Bar and Quesnel. But the map, strangely, didn't show any islands along that part of the Fraser. I'd walked along both banks of the river several times and hadn't seen an island anywhere. But if the 1863 report of the DAILY BRITISH COLONIST was accurate, and I was convinced it was, there had to be an island.

I examined another map of the area. Once again I drew a blank. It was perplexing. Unfolding a third map I perused it. As my eyes scanned the river south of Quesnel I saw it - the unmistakeable dotted contour line of an island on the west side of the river. It hadn't been on any of the other maps but there it was, a low water island. That was why I had missed it during my excursions along the river, it was visible only during the fall and winter, the low water months and my trips had been there either in the spring or summer.

The island was the key to the lost gold and the island was precisely where it should have been. Later, in the fall of 1981, Doug Dodd, an old friend of mine, and I walked down to the island. The island itself wasn't too impressive but the story centering around it was. After five years of searching I was at last able to write the story. This is the story -

In 1863, that banner year for placer gold production in the famous Cariboo District, the mines on Williams Creek were yielding a continuous supply of the royal metal. Claims like the Cameron, Cunningham, Barker, Steele, Aurora and more than a dozen other staggeringly rich claims were producing prodigious amounts of gold while scores of less prominent mines were adding to the steadily mounting total. By the end of that season at least ten tons of gold had been recovered. Some of this hoard was in the hands of the gold kings; Billy Cunningham, "Cariboo" Cameron, "Old Bill" Diller, Billy Barker and several dozen others, but the majority of it was held by the partners and shareholders of less prominent claims.

After being mined, the gold, in raw dust and nugget form, was taken to Victoria, usually by Macdonald's Bank or the Bank of British Columbia. But many miners, not trusting either the banks or express companies, and preferring their own devices, carried their own gold out of the district. This was more often the case at the end of the mining season when most of the wealthier miners, usually owners or shareholders, left the Cariboo to spend the winter months in Victoria where the climate, and assorted other

In 1863 the doomed miners left in boats similar to these pictured on the west side of the Fraser River. Front Street looms up on the far side of the river. This photograph was taken sometime around 1900. (VCA)

amenities, were considerably more inviting.

In November, 1863, after several brutal murders and gold robberies in the Cariboo, forty-one miners, many of them partners or shareholders in the rich Prince of Wales or Tinker claims on renowned Williams Creek, left Camerontown for Quesnellemouth, some sixty miles to the west. Armed and travelling in convoy for mutual protection and bringing out over 400 troy pounds of raw gold, the argonauts made their way overland, arriving at 'The Mouth' several days later. In that colourful one street town they paused to slake their various appetites before embarking on the second leg of their long journey to Victoria.

After spending a few days on rollicking Front Street, the miners commissioned two boats and their French-Canadian steersmen to convey them down the Fraser. Unfortunately, one of their pilots was unfamiliar with the vagaries of the Fraser River south of the mouth of the Quesnel.

Twenty-nine of the argonauts threw their gear into the larger of the two boats, checked their gold pokes, and took their seats. The remaining twelve miners boarded the smaller craft, unaware that it was under the command of an inexperienced boatman.

The two boats pushed off into the current of a rising river. Soon Front Street and its ramshackle buildings receded into the distance. The little flotilla, with the larger craft dropping steadily behind, swept past the mouth of the Quesnel River and continued on down the Fraser.

For a little over two miles, although the current was deceptively fast, the trip was uneventful. But barely a mile later, soon after rounding a sweeping bend, white water was sighted ahead. The larger boat, under an experienced pilot, headed for the slack water on the eastern side of the river. But the thirteen man boat, with a novice in charge, pulled for the opposite shore. It was the first of a series of grievous mistakes by the raw steersman.

While the bigger craft was hugging the relatively safe eastern side of the Fraser, the smaller boat, almost out of control, was careening down the western side. Suddenly a small low island loomed up ahead. Panicking, the new pilot headed for the narrow passage between the island and the steep-sided bank. It was yet another ruinous decision. Near the head of the island the terrified steersman lost all control. A moment later the boat hit a riffle, swung broadside, and immediately turned over flinging everyone aboard into the icy water.

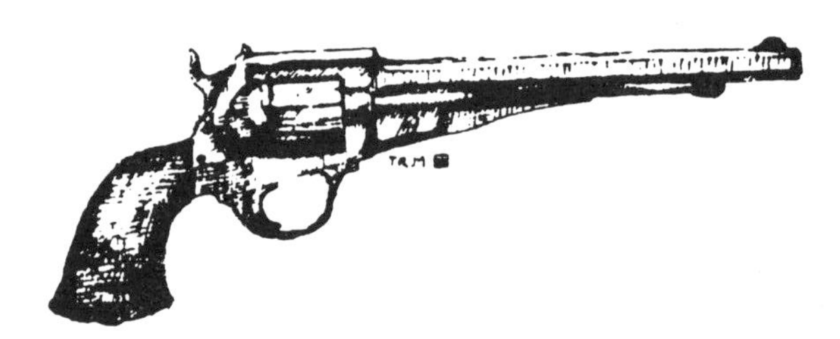

Despite the swiftly running current, two of the drenched miners and the pilot somehow managed to cling to the overturned craft and were rapidly carried off downriver and out of sight. Miraculously, two other argonauts managed to struggle through the rapids to the island. Another, encumbered by more than thirteen pounds of gold in a leather poke tied to his waist, was attempting to gain refuge on the island. But he was gradually losing his battle against the fierce current. Finally, in a desperate effort to save himself; realizing that his precious treasure was a deadly burden, he drew his knife and severed the leather thong which secured his poke to his belt. Immediately his golden anchor plummeted to the bottom. Thus lightened, he managed to fight his way through the last few yards to the island, penniless but alive.

It was a desolate scene. Only a few seconds had elapsed since the accident, but of the thirteen men who had been in the boat only moments before, three were stranded on the tiny, barren island on the western side of the river, three more still desperately holding onto the boat in frigid water far downriver. Of the remaining seven argonauts there was no sign.

The remorseless river had once again taken an awesome toll. The DAILY BRITISH COLONIST had this to say on November 26, 1863:

> "One of the three men who had $2,500 in gold on his person, finding, when within a few feet of the bank, that it was dragging him down, cooly drew his knife and calmly severed the strap which supported the precious yet deadly burden, allowing it to sink to the bottom and thus succeeded in reaching the shore in safety."

Thousands of Cariboo miners returning from the goldfields to Victoria in the fall of 1863 crossed the Fraser on the Alexandra Bridge, shown in this photograph taken soon after construction. (PABC photograph)

All seven of the missing men and their treasure, a total of 2,000 troy ounces of gold, lay at the bottom of the narrow channel where the boat had overturned.

In the same issue of the DAILY BRITISH COLONIST, the names of the dead men and the amount of gold lost were listed:

> "The names of the seven unfortunate men who were drowned are as follows: John Walker, Barnet Rânton, John Robson, Thos. Beatty, John Berth, James Henderson, and - Smith; the first five were from the Prince of Wales Claim, the other two. members of the Tinker Company. The amount of treasure lost was $32,000,...."

While this fatal drama was unfolding, the horror-struck argonauts in the other boat witnessed it. When they saw the small craft capsize, they immediately pulled across the river, ran down the boat and rescued the three men who were still clinging to it. Then they backtracked to the island and took off the remaining argonauts. With the drenched and shivering survivors on board, they continued downriver for another mile and landed at Rich Bar, a mining camp on the eastern side of the river. There the six were given a change of clothes and liquid refreshments. The following day the band returned to Quesnellemouth where news of the catastrophe quickly spread from saloon to saloon. Then, the old miners code, that sometimes fragile and unwritten law that governed most men in the mining camps of the old West, was broken. A number of wretches, realizing that dead men could not hold interests in their old original ground, which was exceptionally rich, immediately set out for Williams Creek to re-stake the dead mens' ground. Among these rogues was the incompetant boatman. The incredible perfidy of these men in breaching the accepted code of conduct was loudly decried. Even in the unrefined goldfields of the Cariboo, it was a shabiness unequalled.

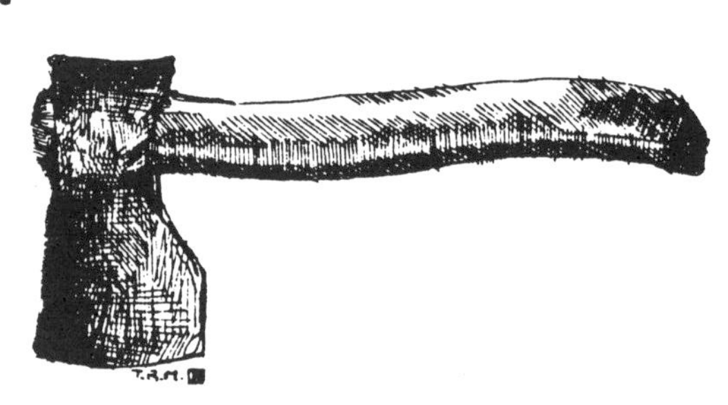

But the opportunists, undeterred by the criticism, continued on to Williams Creek. On December 11th, 1863, the staid COLONIST remarked:

> "Parties had gone to jump the claims belonging to some of the unfortunate men who were recently drowned below the Mouth of Quesnelle, and it was said the Frenchman through whose mismanagement they lost their lives, was one of the would-be jumpers. Commissioner Cox, however, put a stop to the game."

Unfortunately, despite the best efforts of W. G. Cox, the wretches ultimately succeeded in claiming ground on both the Prince of Wales and the Tinker claims. On June 20th, the DAILY BRITISH COLONIST, in another follow-up article commented:

THE

AREA MAP

1. IN NOVEMER of 1863, FORTY-ONE WEALTHY MINERS FROM WILLIAMS CREEK IN THE CARIBOO LEFT THE DIGGINGS TO SPEND THE WINTER IN VICTORIA, V.I. ~

2. AFTER WALKING TO QUESNELLEMOUTH ON THE CARIBOO TRAIL, THEY STOPPED THERE FOR SEVERAL DAYS. THEY THEN HIRED TWO BOATS & THEIR STEERSMEN TO GUIDE THEM DOWN THE FRASER ON THE FIRST LEG of THE LONG TRIP TO VICTORIA ~

3. TWELVE MINERS, MOST of THEM WITH INTERESTS IN THE RICH 'PRINCE of WALES' OR 'TINKER' CLAIMS ON WILLIAMS CREEK, EMBARKED ON A SMALL BOAT IN COMMAND of AN INEXPERIENCED FRENCH-CANADIAN PILOT THE FIRST 3 MILES WERE RUN WITHOUT INCIDENT.

FRASER RIVER

QUESNELLE RIVER

QUESNELLEMOUTH

4. UPON SIGHTING WHITE WATER, HOWEVER, THE TWO CRAFT SEPARATED. THE LARGER BOAT RUNNING DOWN THE EAST SIDE of THE FRASER & THE SMALLER BOAT RUNNING DOWN THE WEST SIDE WHERE IT OVERTURNED JUST ABOVE A SMALL, TREELESS ISLAND.

8. SOON AFTER THE CALAMITY, THE PILOT AND SOME OTHER LOW-PRINCIPLED WRETCHES HURRIED BACK TO WILLIAMS CREEK & STAKED THE CLAIMS of THE DROWNED ARGONAUTS.

9. THE 2,000 TROY OUNCES of LOST GOLD STILL LIES IN THIS AREA. THE LEATHER GOLD POKES WITH THEIR COARSE GOLD WORTH NEARLY $840,000.00 ARE PROBABLY STILL LYING IN SHALLOW WATER JUST ABOVE THE ISLAND.

5. THE 13 MEN WERE THROWN INTO THE RIVER. MOST of THE GOLD THEY WERE CARRYING, SOME 2,000 TROY OUNCES, SECURED IN LEATHER GOLD POKES, WAS PROBABLY LOST WHEN THE BOAT OVERTURNED. ONLY 6 of THE 13 MEN SURVIVED THE TRAGEDY.

7. THE SURVIVORS WERE PUT ASHORE AT RICH BAR AND SOON AFTER RETURNED TO QUESNELLEMOUTH.

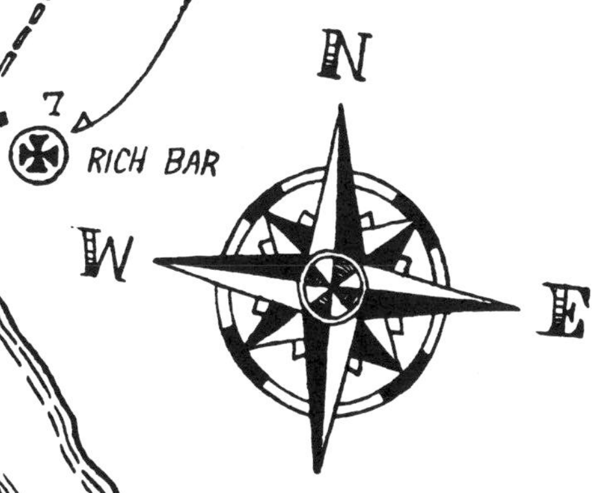

FRASER RIVER

6. THE LARGE BOAT PULLED ACROSS THE RIVER & PICKED UP 3 of THE SURVIVORS CLINGING TO THE OVERTURNED BOAT & THEN PICKED UP THE OTHER 3 STRANDED ON THE LOW WATER ISLAND.

MAP By N.L. BARLEE ~ CANADA WEST MAGAZINE

"Two of the unfortunate men drowned last fall in Fraser river held interests, which are now claimed by parties who recorded them first, immediately after the accident."

For several years longer the Tinker and the Prince of Wales claims continued to yield massive quantities of gold, together producing over one and a half tons of the precious metal. Finally, like all gold claims everywhere, the production eventually dwindled and then ceased.

But the gold lost by the twelve argonauts when their boat went down near that low island in the Fraser, just over three miles south of old Quesnel, has never been recovered. The value of that gold, however, has increased dramatically since that tragic accident in the fall of 1863. Placer gold was worth $16 a crude ounce then. Today, that gold, at least 2,000 ounces and perhaps more, is worth somewhere around $840,000.00.

And it lies there yet, just offshore and probably only a few yards upstream from the low water island on the west side of the Fraser. It is remarkable that although the estimated value of this lost treasure makes it the most valuable of all the documented lost hoards in the province, only a handful of individuals even knew of its existence. Perhaps even more surprising is that since the argonauts' boat capsized more than a century ago, nobody has even attempted to salvage the gold.

EPILOGUE

For years the writer waited for the 'key' lease on the Fraser to be dropped. In 1981, it was finally relinquished and immediately reverted to the Crown. On September 21, 1981, N. L. Barlee and Douglas W. Dodd of nearby Cottonwood, staked a legal fraction Placer Mining Lease on the exact location where the batteaux had capsized in November, 1863. Eight and one half months later a minor official with the Ministry of Energy, Mines and Petroleum Resources in Victoria, B. C. for a number of somewhat debateable reasons saw fit to refuse the application for a placer lease. Contact with the Chief Gold Commissioner in Victoria failed to resolve the issue but he suggested that I contact Mr. H. L. Diemer of the Heritage Conservation Branch. Mr. Diemer realized that the site should be investigated properly and asked that a proposal be submitted to his branch outlining the procedures to be followed during a salvage attempt. In June, 1982, N. L. Barlee, J. M. Duckham and D. W. Dodd delivered a proposal to the Heritage Conservation Branch. In the proposal 34% of the artifacts recovered would be donated by the salvagers to the Provincial Museum as well as a representative amount of nugget gold. By the time this article is published the proposal should be accepted by the Heritage Conservation Branch and a salvage attempt to recover all or part of the sunken hoard will be granted by that branch to the original locators. The salvage attempt on the site will be undertaken sometime in the early fall when the waters of the Fraser subside.

THE ATLIN REGION

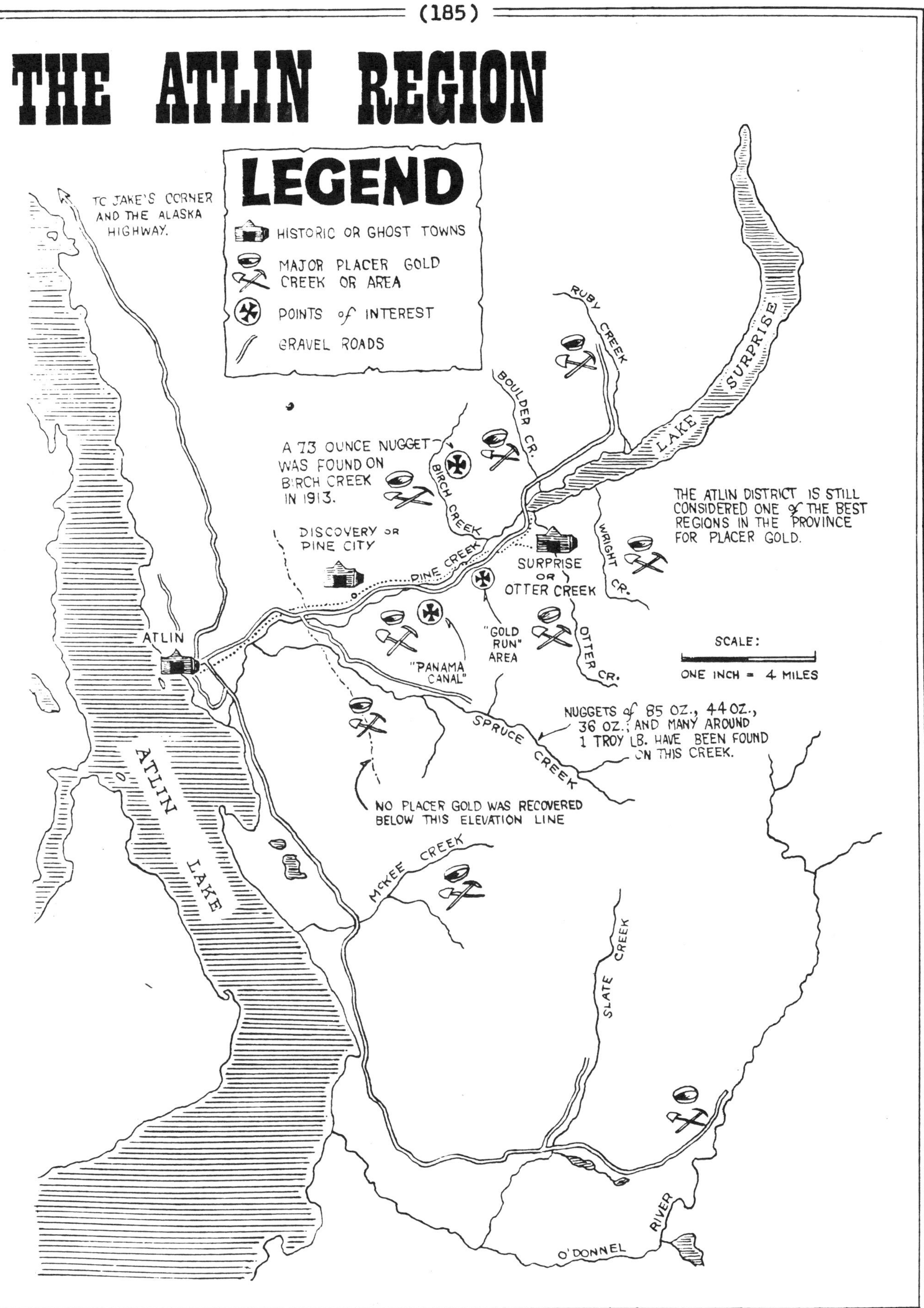

LEGEND
HISTORIC OR GHOST TOWNS
MAJOR PLACER GOLD CREEK OR AREA
POINTS of INTEREST
GRAVEL ROADS
TO JAKE'S CORNER AND THE ALASKA HIGHWAY.
RUBY CREEK
BOULDER CR.
LAKE SURPRISE
A 73 OUNCE NUGGET WAS FOUND ON BIRCH CREEK IN 1913.
BIRCH CREEK
DISCOVERY OR PINE CITY
PINE CREEK
SURPRISE OR OTTER CREEK
WRIGHT CR.
THE ATLIN DISTRICT IS STILL CONSIDERED ONE of THE BEST REGIONS IN THE PROVINCE FOR PLACER GOLD.
ATLIN
"GOLD RUN" AREA
"PANAMA CANAL"
OTTER CR.
SCALE:
ONE INCH = 4 MILES
NUGGETS of 85 OZ., 44 OZ., 36 OZ., AND MANY AROUND 1 TROY LB. HAVE BEEN FOUND ON THIS CREEK.
SPRUCE CREEK
ATLIN LAKE
NO PLACER GOLD WAS RECOVERED BELOW THIS ELEVATION LINE
McKEE CREEK
SLATE CREEK
O'DONNEL RIVER

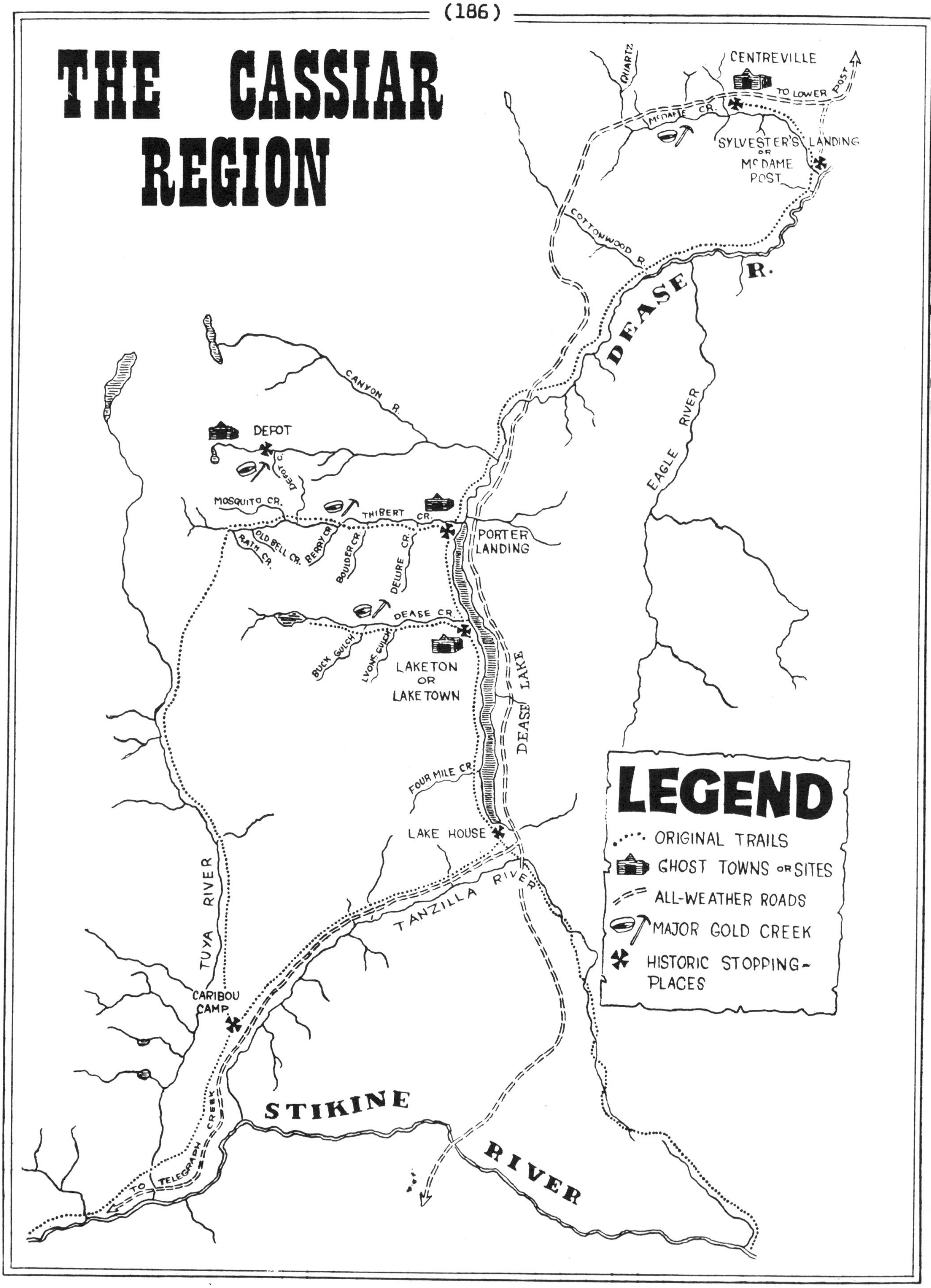

THE CASSIAR REGION

QUARTZ
CENTREVILLE
TO LOWER POST
McDAME CR.
SYLVESTER'S LANDING OR McDAME POST
COTTONWOOD R.
DEASE R.
CANYON R.
DEPOT
DEPOT C.
EAGLE RIVER
MOSQUITO CR.
THIBERT CR.
PORTER LANDING
RATH CR.
OLD BELL CR.
BERRY CR.
BOULDER CR.
DELURE CR.
DEASE CR.
BUCK GULCH
LYONS GULCH
LAKETON OR LAKETOWN
DEASE LAKE
FOUR MILE CR.
LAKE HOUSE
TUYA RIVER
TANZILLA RIVER
CARIBOU CAMP
TELEGRAPH CREEK
TO TELEGRAPH
STIKINE RIVER

LEGEND

ORIGINAL TRAILS
GHOST TOWNS OR SITES
ALL-WEATHER ROADS
MAJOR GOLD CREEK
HISTORIC STOPPING-PLACES

THE OMINECA REGION

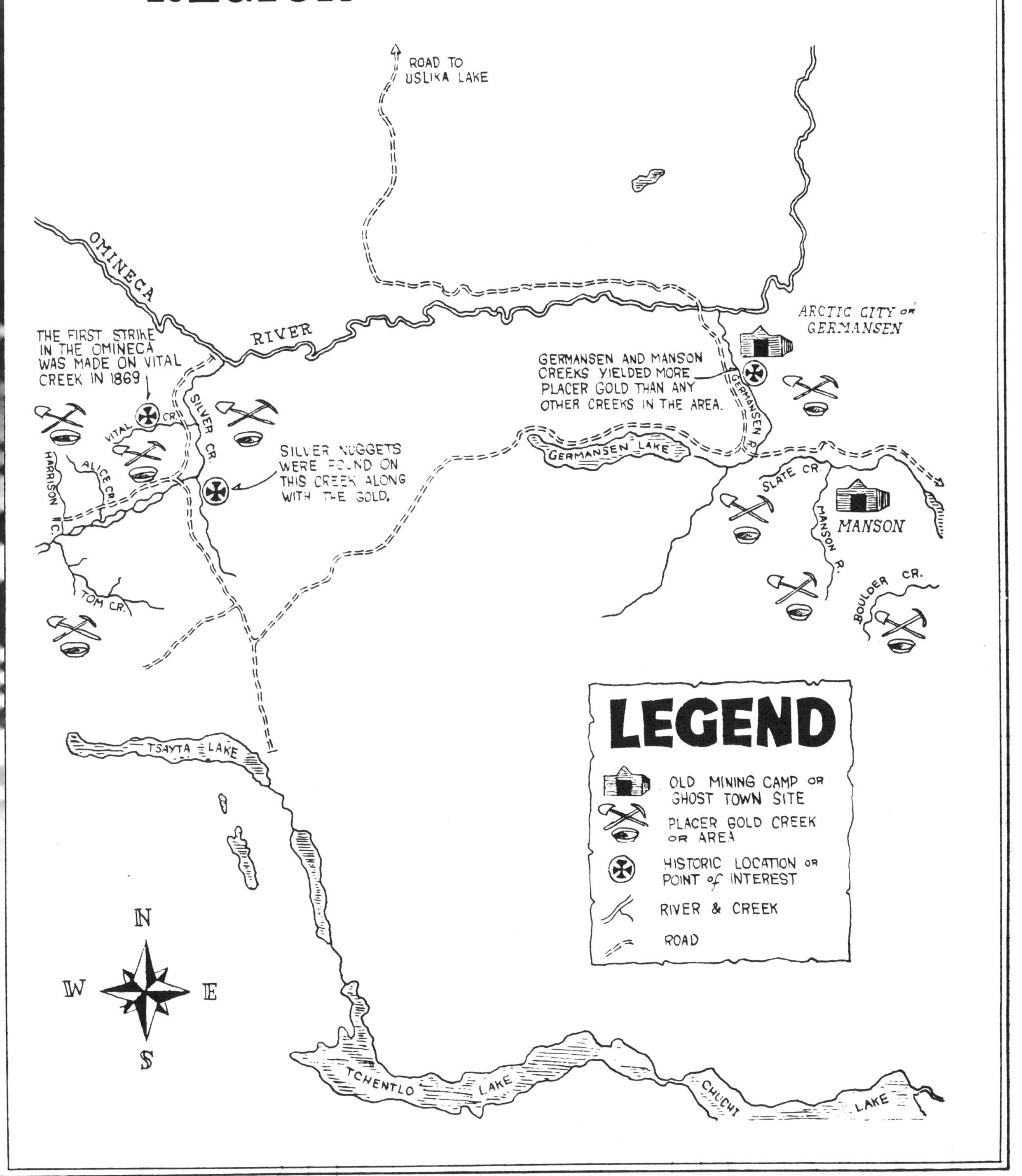

ROAD TO USLIKA LAKE
OMINECA RIVER
THE FIRST STRIKE IN THE OMINECA WAS MADE ON VITAL CREEK IN 1869
VITAL CR.
SILVER CR.
HARRISON C.
ALICE CR.
TOM CR.
SILVER NUGGETS WERE FOUND ON THIS CREEK ALONG WITH THE GOLD.
ARCTIC CITY OR GERMANSEN
GERMANSEN AND MANSON CREEKS YIELDED MORE PLACER GOLD THAN ANY OTHER CREEKS IN THE AREA.
GERMANSEN R.
GERMANSEN LAKE
SLATE CR.
MANSON R.
MANSON
BOULDER CR.
TSAYTA LAKE
LEGEND
OLD MINING CAMP OR GHOST TOWN SITE
PLACER GOLD CREEK OR AREA
HISTORIC LOCATION OR POINT of INTEREST
RIVER & CREEK
ROAD
N
W
E
S
TCHENTLO LAKE
CHUCHI LAKE

THE BIG BEND

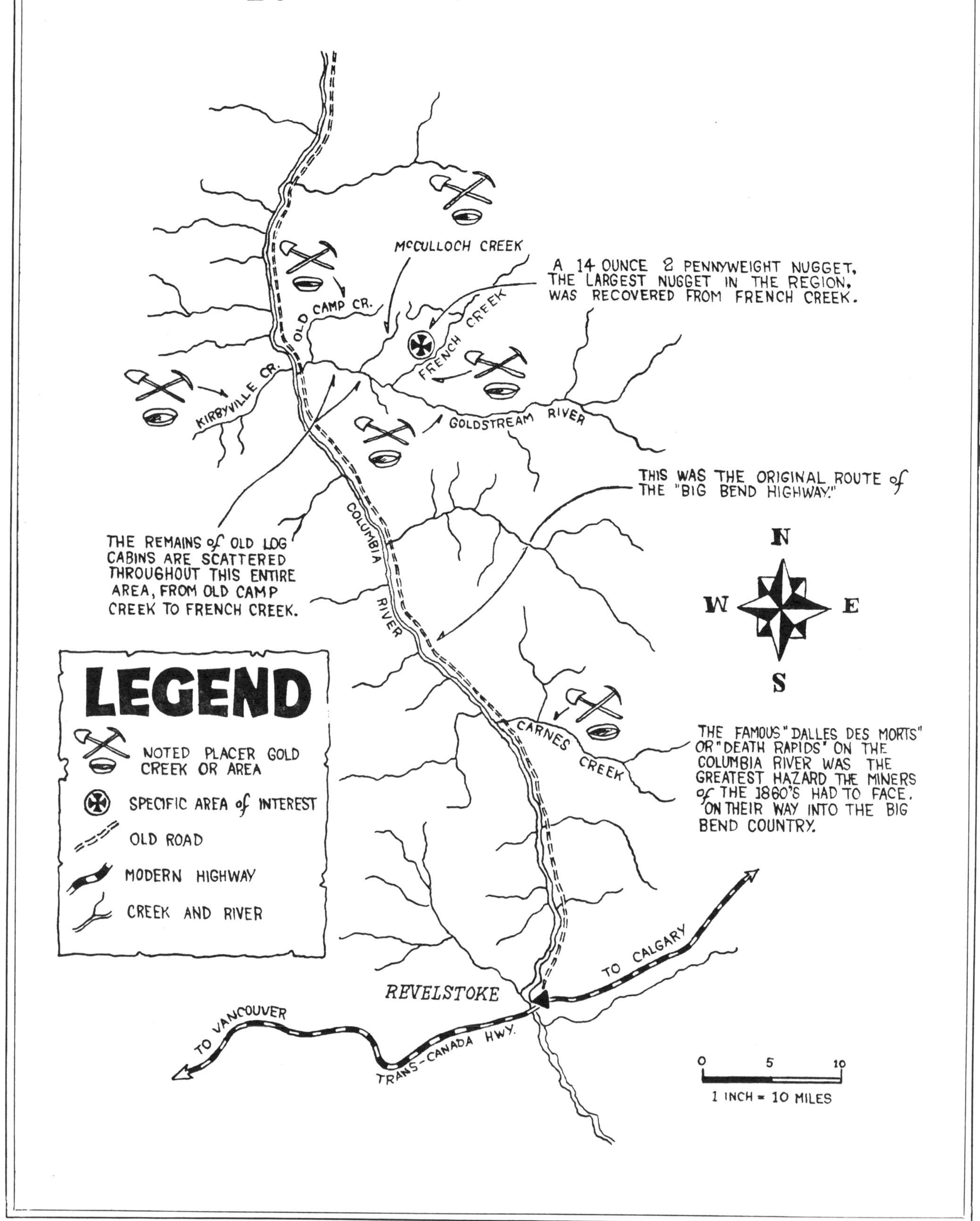
McCULLOCH CREEK
A 14 OUNCE 2 PENNYWEIGHT NUGGET. THE LARGEST NUGGET IN THE REGION, WAS RECOVERED FROM FRENCH CREEK.
OLD CAMP CR.
FRENCH CREEK
KIRBYVILLE CR.
GOLDSTREAM RIVER
THIS WAS THE ORIGINAL ROUTE of THE "BIG BEND HIGHWAY."
THE REMAINS of OLD LOG CABINS ARE SCATTERED THROUGHOUT THIS ENTIRE AREA, FROM OLD CAMP CREEK TO FRENCH CREEK.
COLUMBIA RIVER
N
W
E
S
LEGEND
NOTED PLACER GOLD CREEK OR AREA
SPECIFIC AREA of INTEREST
OLD ROAD
MODERN HIGHWAY
CREEK AND RIVER
CARNES CREEK
THE FAMOUS "DALLES DES MORTS" OR "DEATH RAPIDS" ON THE COLUMBIA RIVER WAS THE GREATEST HAZARD THE MINERS of THE 1860'S HAD TO FACE, ON THEIR WAY INTO THE BIG BEND COUNTRY.
TO CALGARY
REVELSTOKE
TO VANCOUVER
TRANS-CANADA HWY.
0
5
10
1 INCH = 10 MILES

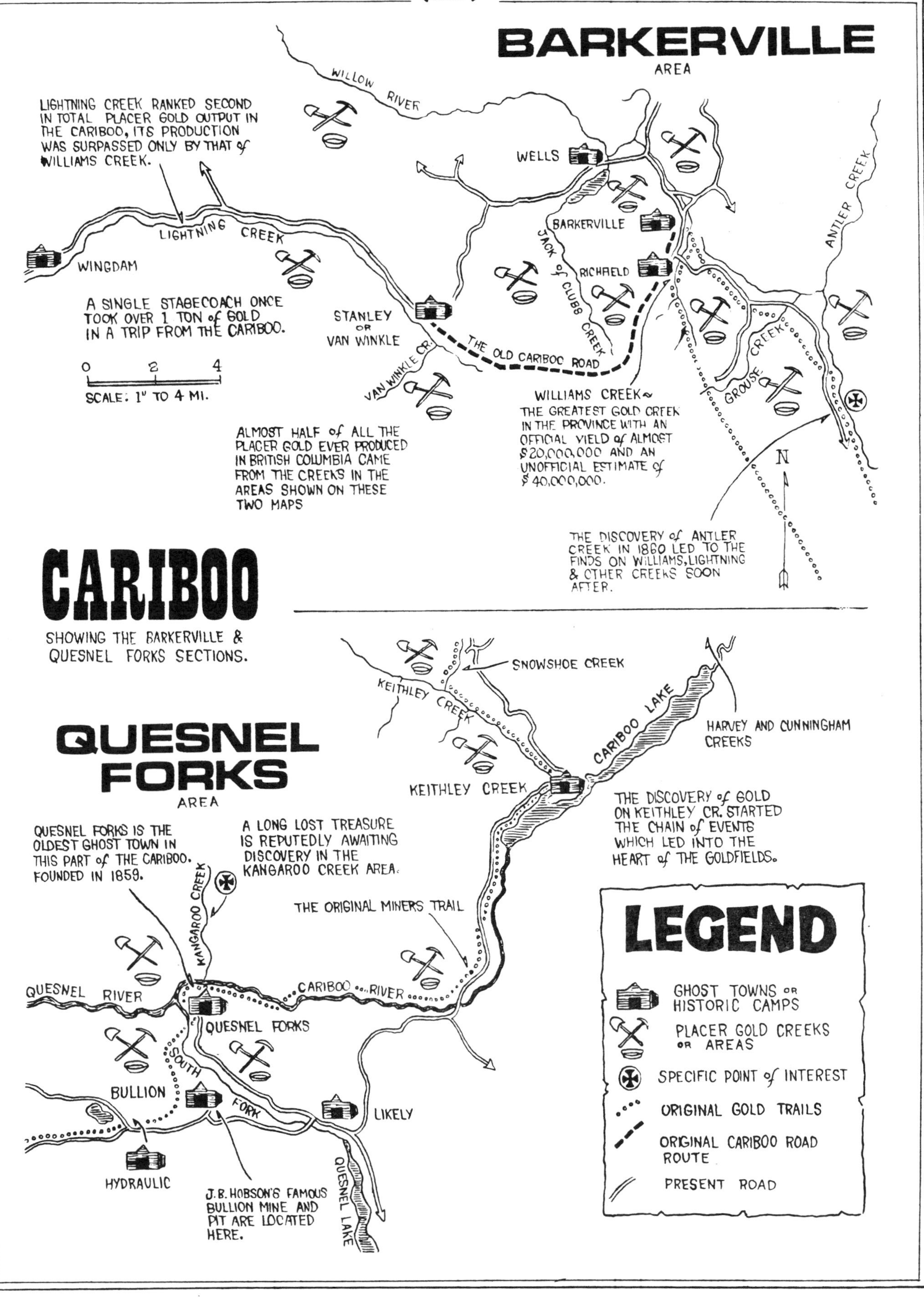
BARKERVILLE
AREA
LIGHTNING CREEK RANKED SECOND IN TOTAL PLACER GOLD OUTPUT IN THE CARIBOO, ITS PRODUCTION WAS SURPASSED ONLY BY THAT of WILLIAMS CREEK.
WILLOW RIVER
WELLS
LIGHTNING CREEK
WINGDAM
BARKERVILLE
JACK of CLUBS CREEK
RICHFIELD
ANTLER CREEK
A SINGLE STAGECOACH ONCE TOOK OVER 1 TON of GOLD IN A TRIP FROM THE CARIBOO.
STANLEY OR VAN WINKLE
THE OLD CARIBOO ROAD
GROUSE CREEK
0 2 4
SCALE: 1" TO 4 MI.
VAN WINKLE CR.
WILLIAMS CREEK~ THE GREATEST GOLD CREEK IN THE PROVINCE WITH AN OFFICIAL YIELD of ALMOST $20,000,000 AND AN UNOFFICIAL ESTIMATE of $40,000,000.
ALMOST HALF of ALL THE PLACER GOLD EVER PRODUCED IN BRITISH COLUMBIA CAME FROM THE CREEKS IN THE AREAS SHOWN ON THESE TWO MAPS
N
THE DISCOVERY of ANTLER CREEK IN 1860 LED TO THE FINDS ON WILLIAMS, LIGHTNING & OTHER CREEKS SOON AFTER.
CARIBOO
SHOWING THE BARKERVILLE & QUESNEL FORKS SECTIONS.
SNOWSHOE CREEK
KEITHLEY CREEK
CARIBOO LAKE
HARVEY AND CUNNINGHAM CREEKS
QUESNEL FORKS
AREA
KEITHLEY CREEK
THE DISCOVERY of GOLD ON KEITHLEY CR. STARTED THE CHAIN of EVENTS WHICH LED INTO THE HEART of THE GOLDFIELDS.
QUESNEL FORKS IS THE OLDEST GHOST TOWN IN THIS PART of THE CARIBOO. FOUNDED IN 1859.
A LONG LOST TREASURE IS REPUTEDLY AWAITING DISCOVERY IN THE KANGAROO CREEK AREA.
KANGAROO CREEK
THE ORIGINAL MINERS TRAIL
QUESNEL RIVER
CARIBOO RIVER
QUESNEL FORKS
SOUTH FORK
BULLION
LIKELY
HYDRAULIC
J.B. HOBSON'S FAMOUS BULLION MINE AND PIT ARE LOCATED HERE.
QUESNEL LAKE
LEGEND
GHOST TOWNS OR HISTORIC CAMPS
PLACER GOLD CREEKS OR AREAS
SPECIFIC POINT of INTEREST
ORIGINAL GOLD TRAILS
ORIGINAL CARIBOO ROAD ROUTE
PRESENT ROAD

EAST KOOTENAY

SHOWING THE WILD HORSE AND PERRY CREEK AREAS

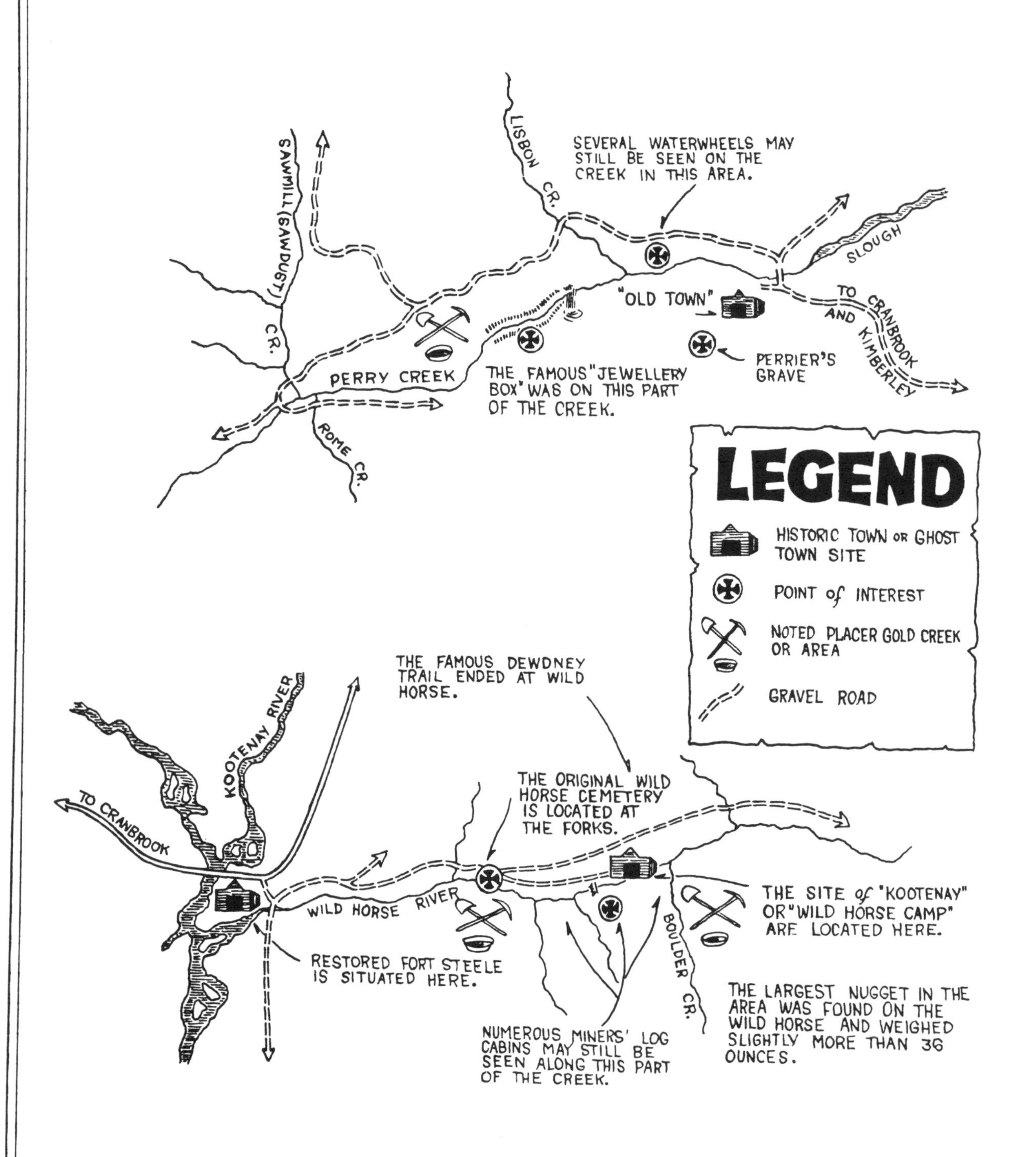
SAWMILL (SAWDUST) CR.
LISBON CR.
SEVERAL WATERWHEELS MAY STILL BE SEEN ON THE CREEK IN THIS AREA.
SLOUGH
"OLD TOWN"
TO CRANBROOK AND KIMBERLEY
PERRY CREEK
THE FAMOUS "JEWELLERY BOX" WAS ON THIS PART OF THE CREEK.
PERRIER'S GRAVE
ROME CR.
LEGEND
HISTORIC TOWN OR GHOST TOWN SITE
POINT of INTEREST
NOTED PLACER GOLD CREEK OR AREA
GRAVEL ROAD
THE FAMOUS DEWDNEY TRAIL ENDED AT WILD HORSE.
KOOTENAY RIVER
TO CRANBROOK
THE ORIGINAL WILD HORSE CEMETERY IS LOCATED AT THE FORKS.
WILD HORSE RIVER
THE SITE of "KOOTENAY" OR "WILD HORSE CAMP" ARE LOCATED HERE.
RESTORED FORT STEELE IS SITUATED HERE.
BOULDER CR.
THE LARGEST NUGGET IN THE AREA WAS FOUND ON THE WILD HORSE AND WEIGHED SLIGHTLY MORE THAN 36 OUNCES.
NUMEROUS MINERS' LOG CABINS MAY STILL BE SEEN ALONG THIS PART OF THE CREEK.